THE
sugarsmart
COOKBOOK

GEORGIA
VAROZZA

HARVEST HOUSE PUBLISHERS
EUGENE, OREGON

Cover by Dugan Design Group

Cover Image © roggozub, pilipphoto, myviewpoint / Fotolia

All oven temperatures are given in degrees Fahrenheit.

THE SUGAR SMART COOKBOOK

Copyright © 2017 by Georgia Varozza
Published by Harvest House Publishers
Eugene, Oregon 97402
www.harvesthousepublishers.com

ISBN 978-0-7369-7139-3 (pbk.)
ISBN 978-0-7369-7140-9 (eBook)

Library of Congress Cataloging-in-Publication Data

Names: Varozza, Georgia, author.
Title: The sugar smart cookbook / Georgia Varozza.
Description: Eugene, Oregon : Harvest House Publishers, [2017]
Identifiers: LCCN 2017008139 (print) | LCCN 2017009245 (ebook) | ISBN 9780736971393 (pbk.) | ISBN 9780736971409 (ebook)
Subjects: LCSH: Cooking. | Low-calorie diet—Recipes. | LCGFT: Cookbooks.
Classification: LCC TX714 .V36 2017 (print) | LCC TX714 (ebook) | DDC 641.5/6383—dc23
LC record available at https://lccn.loc.gov/2017008139

Printed in China

17 18 19 20 21 22 23 24 25 / RDS-KBD / 10 9 8 7 6 5 4 3 2 1

To Walker, Travis, Logan, Sara, Crystalynn,
Audrey, Asher, Easton, Alexis, and Everett

I love you more than the whole wide world
…then, now, and always

CONTENTS

BREADS, CRACKERS, AND MUFFINS

BREAKFAST AND BRUNCH

DESSERTS

GRAINS AND NOODLES

LUNCHES AND LIGHT FARE

MAIN DISHES AND CASSEROLES

SALADS AND SALAD DRESSINGS

SOUPS AND STEWS

VEGETABLES AND SIDES

IS EATING A
SUGAR-SMART DIET
FOR YOU?

Some years ago, troubled that I had gained unwanted weight, I spoke with my doctor about my concerns. She advised me to begin a low-fat eating regimen. I started researching food options available to me, bought several cookbooks to help inspire me to cook a bit differently, and scoured the grocery store shelves for low-fat alternatives to my normal fare. I was disciplined—and continued to slowly gain weight. After a frustrating few years, I began to take a serious look into the ingredients of what I was eating. I realized that much of my so-called low-fat diet was laced with large amounts of hidden sugar and other ingredients that were a mystery to me. I began to put two and two together.

After lots of thought, and with some trepidation, I threw out the expert advice and simply ate the way I intuitively felt was best for me. I decided to eat unprocessed food as much as possible, and I stopped keeping the cookie jar full all the time (much to my kids' chagrin). It wasn't long before I felt better and had energy throughout the day. And I noticed that my kids had steady energy as well.

I was on to something.

For years, health experts, doctors, and nutritionists have advocated a low-fat diet as a way to lose or maintain a healthy weight, feel better, and stave off health problems. But, in general, people in the developed areas of the world keep getting fatter—and subsequently unhealthier. During this same time, changes in our eating habits have taken place. Processed foods have made big inroads into the Western diet, and the amount of sugar we eat has risen dramatically. Somewhere along the way, we had a disconnect. With evidence piling up as to how our current eating patterns were creating problems for us, still we went on eating the same way as we have for years.

Do you or members of your family wish they could lose a few pounds? Do you or your loved ones ever crave a "sugar fix"? Have you or a loved one ever binged on sugar, refined carbohydrates, or processed food? The answer to these questions is likely yes. Perhaps, then, high-fat eating isn't the only culprit in our population's weight gain. Recent studies indicate that the spike in sugar consumption has led to problems such as obesity, high blood sugar levels, type 2 diabetes, heart disease, hypertension, hypoglycemia, tooth decay, and mood swings.

I think it's time to lose the sugar in our diets. Now, I'm not advocating going completely sugar-free. That wouldn't be enjoyable or even doable for most of us. Because let's face it: Sugar tastes good. But there is much we can do to reduce our sugar intake and keep sugar in its proper place—as a treat to be eaten in smaller quantities.

I firmly believe we need to get back into our kitchens and do our own meal preparation, where *we* decide what ingredients go into the food we serve to our families and where no hidden surprises lurk. Of course, I realize people are busy. That's why many of the recipes in this book take minimal labor—but the results are delicious. And better yet? You'll know exactly what you are feeding your family, and you'll be on the road to making healthier food decisions for those you love. Concentrate on salads and vegetables, with a smaller portion of lean meats, poultry, or fish. Make your carbohydrates the smallest portion on your plate, and learn to enjoy whole grains instead of processed. Teach your taste buds to savor the natural sweetness of fruit. And, when you do decide to have dessert, keep your portions realistic, eat slowly, and enjoy the special treat. You can do this!

Is eating a sugar-smart diet for you and your family? The answer is yes. And may I also say that I think you and your loved ones will hardly notice the difference. Add to that the peace of mind you'll gain by knowing that you are making the smart choice for your family, and you may agree with me that this way of eating will be worth every moment.

Blessings,

Georgia Varozza

> *Dear friend, I pray that you may enjoy good health*
> *and that all may go well with you,*
> *even as your soul is getting along well.*
>
> 3 JOHN 2

BREADS, CRACKERS, AND MUFFINS

Applesauce Nut Bread

1½ cups whole wheat pastry flour (or regular whole wheat flour.)
1 tsp. baking powder
1 tsp. baking soda
1 tsp. salt
1 tsp. cinnamon
½ tsp. nutmeg
1 cup rolled oats
½ cup walnuts, chopped
½ cup raisins
⅓ cup shortening
½ cup brown sugar
2 eggs
1 cup unsweetened applesauce
½ cup milk

Preheat the oven to 350°.

In a large mixing bowl, sift together the flour, baking powder, baking soda, salt, cinnamon, and nutmeg. Stir in the rolled oats, walnuts, and raisins.

In another bowl, cream together the shortening and brown sugar. Add the eggs and beat until light and fluffy. Blend in the applesauce and milk.

Add the creamed mixture to the dry ingredients and beat for 30 seconds. Although the batter will be lumpy, don't overbeat it. Spoon batter into a large, greased loaf pan and bake at 350° for 50 to 60 minutes. Let the bread cool a bit before attempting to slice it. When completely cooled, you can wrap it in plastic wrap to store for a day or two. In fact, it tastes better the next day.

Yields 1 loaf or about 12 servings.

Baked Whole Wheat Pita Chips

2 T. olive oil
¼ tsp. garlic powder
2 large whole wheat pitas (about 7-inch diameter)
½ tsp. coarse salt

Preheat the oven to 350°.

Combine the olive oil and garlic powder in a small bowl.

Cut the pitas into 8 wedges each and then gently split the pockets to make 2 triangles. (You may need to split the pockets with a butter knife.)

Brush both sides of the triangles with a light coating of the olive oil mixture, and place the chips on a baking sheet in a single layer. Using the salt sparingly, sprinkle it over the chips.

Bake for 10 minutes. Turn the chips so the second side is up, and continue baking for another 5 to 10 minutes or until the chips are crisp and lightly browned.

Yields 32 chips.

Banana Strawberry Muffins

1¼ cups whole wheat flour
2 tsp. baking powder
½ tsp. cinnamon
¼ tsp. nutmeg
¼ tsp. salt
1 T. butter, melted and cooled
1 egg
1½ tsp. vanilla
1 very ripe banana, peeled and mashed (about ½ cup)
2 T. honey
¼ cup plain Greek yogurt
¾ cup strawberries, diced

Preheat the oven to 325°.

Grease 8 muffin cups (use vegetable shortening, butter, or non-stick cooking spray).

In a medium mixing bowl, whisk together the flour, baking powder, cinnamon, nutmeg, and salt.

In another, larger mixing bowl, beat together the butter, egg, and vanilla. Stir in the mashed banana, honey, and Greek yogurt. Mix until well blended. Add the flour mixture to the wet ingredients and stir just until blended. Don't overmix. Fold in strawberries.

Spoon batter evenly into the prepared muffin cups and bake for 22 to 25 minutes or until a toothpick inserted into the center of a muffin comes out clean. Cool in the muffin tin for about 5 minutes before removing to continue cooling on a wire rack.

Serves 8.

Bran Muffins

1½ cups organic bran cereal (such as Nature's Path Organic Smart Bran Cereal)
1⅓ cups milk
1 egg
2 T. oil
1¼ cups flour (I use a combination of whole wheat and oat flour and measure scant portions.)
1 T. baking powder
½ tsp. salt
2 T. sugar
½ cup raisins

Preheat the oven to 375°.

In a mixing bowl, combine the cereal and milk; let stand for 5 minutes. Add the egg and oil and beat well by hand. Add the flour, baking powder, salt, sugar, and raisins and mix by hand until the dry ingredients are moistened, but don't overmix.

Spoon the batter into greased or paper-lined muffin cups and bake for 20 to 25 minutes. Cool in the tins for a few minutes before removing the muffins to a wire cooling rack.

Yields 12 to 16 muffins.

Cheddar Cheese Crisps

Cheddar cheese, shredded, 1 tablespoon per crisp

Preheat the oven to 375°.

Line a cookie sheet with a silicone baking mat or parchment paper. Drop piles of about a tablespoon of cheese onto the prepared cookie sheet.

Bake for 10 to 15 minutes, watching the crisps carefully after about 10 minutes—they need to begin browning on the edges and look crisp. (If you take them out too soon, they'll still be melty. But wait too long, and they'll be dark brown.)

Remove the cheese crisps from the oven and allow them to cool for about 10 minutes before removing them from the pan.

These are good alone, with dip, or broken up and tossed in a green salad.

Yield varies.

Cheddar Cheese Puffs

1 cup cheddar cheese, shredded
½ cup flour
¼ cup butter, room temperature
½ tsp. mustard powder

Preheat the oven to 400°.

In a mixing bowl, mix all ingredients until well blended. Roll into 1-inch balls and place at least 1 inch apart on an ungreased baking sheet. Bake for 12 to 15 minutes or until lightly browned.

These are great served in lieu of bread with soup, stews, or salads.

Yields approximately 12 puffs.

Chocolate Banana Muffins

1½ cups whole wheat flour
1 tsp. baking soda
¼ tsp. salt
3 bananas
¼ cup honey
1 T. vanilla
1 T. oil
1 egg
½ cup plain Greek yogurt
1 T. milk
½ cup chocolate chips

Preheat the oven to 350°.

Grease 12 muffin cups (or use nonstick cooking spray).

In a large mixing bowl, combine the flour, baking soda, and salt.

In another bowl, beat together the bananas, honey, vanilla, oil, egg, yogurt, and milk until well combined and smooth (or use a blender). Add the dry ingredients to the wet ingredients and mix just until combined. Fold in the chocolate chips.

Spoon batter into the muffin cups and bake for 20 to 25 minutes or until a toothpick inserted into the middle of a muffin comes out clean. Cool muffins in the tin for 5 minutes and then remove them to a wire rack to cool completely.

Serves 12.

Graham Crackers

2 cups whole wheat flour
2 tsp. baking powder
¼ tsp. salt
¼ cup brown sugar
½ cup (1 stick) butter
2 T. honey
2 T. milk
Dash of vanilla
Dash of cinnamon (optional)

Preheat the oven to 375°.

Combine all ingredients to make dough. Turn out onto a cookie sheet and roll into a square or rectangle about ⅛-inch thick. Deeply score dough into 2- to 3-inch squares. Bake for 8 minutes. (Watch carefully for the last few minutes to make sure they don't burn!) Allow to cool slightly before cutting through crackers on the score lines.

Yields about 2 dozen crackers, depending on thickness of dough and size of crackers.

Nothing-but-Corn Bread

2 eggs
2 cups buttermilk
2 cups cornmeal, fine grind
1 tsp. baking soda
1 tsp. salt
1 T. butter, for greasing frying pan

Preheat the oven to 350°.

In a medium mixing bowl, whisk the eggs until they are thoroughly combined. Whisk in the buttermilk, and then add the cornmeal, baking soda, and salt.

Butter a frying pan (cast iron works best), pour in the batter, and bake at 350° for about 45 minutes or until a fork inserted just off center comes out clean.

Serves 8.

Oat and Wheat Crackers

1½ cups rolled oats
1 cup whole wheat flour
1 T. flaxseed
1 tsp. salt
½ tsp. garlic powder
1½ tsp. dried rosemary
2 T. olive oil
3 T. plain applesauce
½ cup water (You may need a bit more.)
Coarse salt (optional)

Preheat the oven to 350°.

Process the oats in a food processor or blender until it is flour. (A few remaining small pieces are fine.)

In a large mixing bowl, whisk together the oat flour, whole wheat flour, flaxseed, salt, garlic powder, and rosemary. Add the olive oil, applesauce, and water and mix until a soft dough forms. (You may need to add a bit more water, a teaspoon at a time, if the dough seems too dry.)

Cut or tear the dough into two equal pieces. Roll out each half on a silicone baking mat or parchment paper to a square about ⅛-inch thick. Lightly sprinkle salt over the dough if desired. Score the crackers with a sharp knife, making squares or rectangles. Bake for 10 to 15 minutes until the crackers are just barely brown, checking every minute after the 10-minute mark. You might need to remove the outside crackers and then bake the center crackers a minute or two longer.

Allow the crackers to cool before breaking them apart at the score lines.

Yield varies, depending on size of individual crackers.

Pumpkin Cranberry Muffins

1 cup whole wheat flour
½ cups oat flour (or grind oatmeal yourself in a food processor or blender)
1 tsp. baking soda
½ tsp. baking powder
½ tsp. cinnamon
¼ tsp. salt
¼ tsp. nutmeg
¼ cup brown sugar
1 cup canned pumpkin
½ cup buttermilk
1 T. vanilla
2 T. butter, melted and cooled
1 egg
⅓ cup dried cranberries, no sugar added
¼ cup pistachios

Preheat the oven to 375°.

Grease muffin cups or use paper liners.

In a medium mixing bowl, whisk together the wheat flour, oat flour, baking soda, baking powder, cinnamon, salt, nutmeg, and brown sugar.

In a separate bowl, beat together the pumpkin, buttermilk, vanilla, butter, and egg.

Combine the wet and dry ingredients and mix just until blended. Don't overmix. Fold in the cranberries and pistachios. Spoon the batter into the prepared muffin cups and bake for 22 to 25 minutes or until a toothpick inserted in the center of a muffin comes out clean.

Yields 12 to 15 muffins.

Wheat Bran Muffins

1½ cups wheat bran
1 cup milk
1½ cups whole wheat flour
2 T. sugar
1 tsp. salt
1 T. baking powder
1 egg
¼ cup oil
2 T. molasses
¼ cup diced apples or whole blueberries (or use dried fruit)

Preheat the oven to 400°.

Soak the wheat bran in the milk for 5 minutes.

In a large mixing bowl, combine the flour, sugar, salt, and baking powder.

In a small bowl, whisk together the egg, oil, and molasses.

Add the wheat bran and milk mixture to the dry ingredients and stir with a large spoon just until most of the dry ingredients are moistened. Add the egg mixture and fruit pieces and stir again just until mixed.

Spoon muffin batter into greased or paper-lined muffin cups and bake at 400° for 20 to 25 minutes.

Yields 12 to 16 muffins.

Wheat Muffins

1 cup whole wheat flour
1 cup white flour
1 tsp. baking soda
¼ tsp. salt
3 T. butter, melted
¼ cup brown sugar
1 cup buttermilk
1 egg

Preheat the oven to 350°.

In a large mixing bowl, combine the flours, baking soda, and salt.

In another bowl, mix the butter, brown sugar, buttermilk, and egg; add to the flour mixture. Mix just until blended. Don't overmix.

Pour batter into greased muffin cups and bake for 15 to 20 minutes or until done.

Yields about 12 muffins.

Whole Grain Buttermilk Crackers with Cumin

1¼ cups whole wheat flour
½ cup wheat germ
¼ cup sunflower seeds
1 tsp. ground cumin
½ tsp. baking powder
½ tsp. baking soda
½ tsp. salt
3 T. cold butter, diced (see note below)
½ cup buttermilk
Coarse salt for sprinkling

Note: I usually dice the butter into small pieces and set it in the refrigerator until needed so it stays well chilled.

Preheat the oven to 350°.

In a food processor, pulse flour, wheat germ, sunflower seeds, cumin, baking powder, baking soda, and salt until well blended. Add the butter and process until mixture resembles coarse crumbles. With the machine running, gradually add the buttermilk and process until the dough comes together and looks fully mixed and moist. Transfer the dough to a lightly floured work surface and allow to rest for 5 minutes.

Roll the dough into a rectangle about ⅛- to ¼-inch thick. Sprinkle the dough lightly with coarse salt and then roll or pat the surface gently to help the salt adhere to the dough.

Cut the dough into squares (about 2 to 3 inches on each side) and carefully transfer the crackers to ungreased baking sheets. Pierce each cracker several times with the tines of a fork.

Bake for 15 to 16 minutes or until the crackers are hard but not too dark. Transfer to wire racks to cool.

Yields vary depending on size and thickness of crackers.

Whole Wheat Cheddar Cheese Crackers

1 cup whole wheat flour
5 T. cold butter, cut into small chunks (about 10 pieces total)
1½ cups sharp cheddar cheese, grated
⅛ tsp. onion powder

Combine all of the ingredients in a food processor and blend until the mixture comes together in a ball.

Roll the dough ball into a log about an inch in diameter. Wrap tightly in plastic wrap and refrigerate for an hour.

When ready to bake, preheat the oven to 350°.

Using a sharp knife so the cuts are clean, slice the log into very thin rounds (no thicker than ¼ inch—the thinner, the better). Place them on a baking sheet lined with parchment paper or a silicone baking mat and bake for 8 to 15 minutes, depending on how thick they are.

Yields vary, but I usually get about 20 rounds.

Whole Wheat Crackers

2 cups whole wheat flour
1 tsp. salt
½ cup sesame seeds
¼ cup wheat germ
¼ cup oil
¼ cup Parmesan cheese, grated
¼ cup water (slightly more may be needed)

Preheat the oven to 350°.

Combine all ingredients. Add enough water to hold dough together. Roll out on a floured board (thinner dough makes crisper crackers) and cut into desired shapes.

Bake on an ungreased cookie sheet for 8 to 10 minutes.

Yields vary.

Whole Wheat Flaxseed Bread

3 cups warm water (about 100°)
2 T. active dry yeast
5 to 6 cups whole wheat flour, divided
3 T. honey
3 T. oil
1½ cups flaxseed meal
⅓ cup raw sunflower seeds
2 T. poppy seeds
2 tsp. salt

In a large mixing bowl, combine the warm water and yeast; let set for about 10 minutes or until bubbly. Add 2 cups of the whole wheat flour, honey, and oil, and stir vigorously with a large wooden spoon for several minutes.

Now add the flaxseed meal, sunflower seeds, poppy seeds, and salt and mix. Keep adding whole wheat flour until a rough dough forms and pulls away from the sides of the bowl.

Then, turn the dough out on a clean work surface that has been liberally floured and knead for about 10 minutes.

Place the ball of dough in a large greased bowl, cover with a damp cloth, and let rise in a warm place until doubled, about 1½ hours.

Punch down the dough, divide in half, and let rest, covered with the cloth, for 5 minutes.

Shape dough into two loaves and place them in greased loaf pans. Cover and let rise again for about 1 hour.

Bake in a preheated 375° oven for 30 minutes. Remove from loaf pans and cool before slicing.

Yields 2 loaves.

BREAKFAST AND BRUNCH

Apple Cinnamon Granola

4 cups rolled oats
½ cup unsweetened coconut
1 cup nuts, finely chopped
½ cup sesame seeds
¾ tsp. salt
1 tsp. cinnamon
⅓ cup honey
⅓ cup oil
½ tsp. vanilla
1 cup dried apples, finely chopped

Preheat the oven to 350°.

Combine the oats, coconut, nuts, sesame seeds, salt, and cinnamon in a large mixing bowl. In another bowl, combine the honey, oil, and vanilla and then add to the dry ingredients. Mix thoroughly.

Spread out on two parchment-lined baking sheets (or use silicone baking mats) and bake for 20 to 25 minutes, stirring occasionally. By using the parchment or silicone mats, more of the honey mixture will stick to the oats instead of sticking to the baking sheets, which means your granola will clump nicely and taste better.

Cool granola completely and then gently mix in the dried apple pieces.

Store in a tightly covered container or large plastic freezer bags with as much of the air taken out as possible. It should stay fresh for up to two months.

Yields about 2 quarts.

Bacon, Egg, and Cheese Casserole

Note: Put this casserole together the night before and bake it in the morning.

½ lb. bacon
6 slices whole wheat bread
1 cup cheddar cheese
6 eggs
2 cups milk
½ tsp. salt
¼ tsp. pepper

Fry bacon until crisp and then crumble into pieces; set aside.

Cut bread into cubes and place in a well-buttered 2-quart casserole dish. Cube or shred cheese and layer on top of bread cubes.

In a mixing bowl, beat eggs, milk, salt, and pepper. Pour over the bread and cheese. Sprinkle bacon pieces on top. Cover and refrigerate overnight.

In the morning, remove the casserole from the refrigerator, take off the cover, and let it sit for about 30 minutes while your oven is preheating to 350°. Bake for 50 to 60 minutes or until puffed up and golden.

Serves 6.

Bacon and Swiss Cheese Breakfast Strata

1 small onion, chopped
½ green bell pepper, chopped
½ red bell pepper, chopped
4 slices bacon, chopped
4 slices whole wheat bread, cut into ½-inch cubes
⅓ cup shredded Swiss cheese
4 eggs
1¾ cups milk
1 T. Dijon mustard
¼ tsp. black pepper

Lightly grease a large skillet or use a conditioned cast-iron pan and heat on medium. Add the chopped onion and bell peppers and sauté until the vegetables are almost done. Add the bacon and continue to cook, stirring occasionally, for 3 more minutes. Remove from heat and add the bread cubes.

Spread the mixture evenly in a buttered 11x17-inch baking dish.

In a medium mixing bowl, whisk together the cheese, eggs, milk, Dijon mustard, and pepper; pour evenly over the bread mixture. If you are baking it now, let it stand for 20 minutes before baking (see below). If you are making it the night before, cover the strata with plastic wrap and refrigerate overnight.

When ready to bake, remove from refrigerator, discard the plastic wrap, and let stand 20 minutes while oven is preheating to 375°. Bake the strata for 35 to 40 minutes or until a knife inserted into the center of the casserole comes out clean. Let stand for 5 to 10 minutes before serving.

Serves 8.

BREAKFAST AND BRUNCH

Baked Chili Rellenos

2 cans (4 or 4½ ounces each) whole green chilies, drained
1½ cups Monterey Jack cheese, shredded
½ cup cheddar cheese, shredded
5 eggs
½ cup milk
1 T. flour
½ tsp. salt
¼ tsp. pepper
Several drops of hot sauce
Paprika for sprinkling

Note: If you don't have whole chilies, you can substitute two cans (4 ounces each) of chopped green chilies, drained.

Preheat the oven to 375°.

Lightly butter or grease a 8 x 8-inch square baking dish. Cut the chilies in half lengthwise and remove seeds. Place half of the chilies in the bottom of the baking dish.

In a bowl, mix the cheeses. Place half of the cheese mixture on top of the layer of chilies in the baking dish. Repeat the layers with the remainder of the chilies and cheese.

In another bowl, beat the eggs. Add the milk, flour, salt, pepper, and hot sauce. Pour egg mixture over the chilies and cheese. Sprinkle paprika on top.

Bake uncovered for 25 to 30 minutes. Remove from the oven and allow to rest for several minutes before cutting.

Serves 4 to 6.

Baked Eggs in a Muffin Tin

Note: You can make up to a dozen eggs at once if you have a 12-hole muffin tin. These are quick and easy to prepare, and the entire family's breakfast is done at the same time.

For each serving:

Softened butter
1 T. shredded cheese (cheddar, jack, Parmesan, etc.)
2 T. precooked meat, diced (ham, bacon, sausage, etc.)
1 egg
Salt and pepper to taste

Preheat the oven to 350°.

Grease muffin cup with softened butter. Add the shredded cheese and precooked meat and then crack the egg into the cup over the meat and cheese. Salt and pepper to taste.

Using a baking pan with sides that are slightly larger than the muffin tin, layer the bottom of the pan with a folded kitchen towel or several layers of paper towels and then place the filled tin on the cushion. Carefully pour boiling water into the baking pan so the water level comes about halfway up the sides of the muffin cups. Immediately place in the oven and bake for 14 to 25 minutes, depending on how hard you like your eggs.

Serve immediately, either alone or on top of a piece of toast, slices of fresh tomatoes, or English muffin.

Basic Granola

6 cups rolled oats
2 cups (any combination) raw walnuts and sunflower seeds
½ to ¾ cup honey, depending on taste
1 T. salt (scant)
¾ cup oil
½ cup water
3 tsp. vanilla
2 cups raisins
2 cups toasted wheat germ

Preheat the oven to 300°.

Combine all ingredients except for raisins and wheat germ. Spread in thin layer on large baking pans. Bake for 1 hour, stirring occasionally.

Cool completely and then add the raisins and wheat germ.

You can also add unsweetened coconut or dried fruit (chopped).

Store in airtight container or large food storage or freezer bags with as much air squeezed out as possible. It should stay fresh for about two months.

Yields about 3 quarts.

Note: Even though this granola recipe uses ½ cup of honey, it's sweet enough on its own that you won't need to add any other sweetener when it's time to eat, and the recipe makes a large batch.

Also, did you know there is no need to preheat the oven if your baking time is an hour or longer?

Berry Peach Smoothie

1 handful torn spinach, kale, or other greens
1 peach, pitted and chunked
½ cup blueberries
½ cup strawberries
4 ice cubes
1 cup milk (regular, coconut, almond, or soy)

Place all ingredients in a blender, and blend on high until smooth.

This is a great way to get a serving of healthy greens into your kids' diets without fuss.

Serves 1.

Breakfast Sausage and Spinach Frittata

1 T. butter
2 slices whole wheat bread, torn up
½ lb. sausage, browned and drained
²/₃ cup cheddar cheese, shredded
½ cup fresh spinach, chopped
4 eggs
½ cup milk
Salt and pepper to taste

Melt the butter in a heavy skillet or cast-iron fry pan that has a lid and turn to cover the entire bottom of pan. Add torn bread and stir a bit to distribute evenly and completely cover the bottom of the pan. Sprinkle on sausage, cheese, and spinach.

Whisk together the eggs and milk that have been seasoned with salt and pepper and pour over the sausage mixture. Cover and cook on medium-low heat for about 15 minutes or until the eggs are set. (If the bottom seems to be cooking too fast, turn down the heat slightly.)

Serves 4 to 6.

Buckwheat Pancakes

2 cups buckwheat flour
2 eggs, beaten
1 tsp. sugar
2 tsp. baking powder
⅛ tsp. salt
1½ cups milk
½ cup water

Combine all ingredients. Drop the batter on a well-greased hot griddle and cook the pancakes until they are brown, and then turn and cook the other side.

Serves 6 to 8.

Note: Buckwheat has a nutty, robust flavor. If you prefer, you can use 1 cup buckwheat flour and 1 cup whole wheat flour for a slightly less distinct taste.

Cherry Ginger Smoothie

1 banana, peeled and chunked
½ cup frozen strawberries
1 large kale leaf, torn
¼ to ½ tsp. ginger, depending on taste
1½ cups tart cherry juice, well chilled
1 tsp. honey (optional)

Place all ingredients in a blender and blend until smooth.

Seves 1.

Citrus Smoothie

1 orange, peeled and sectioned
¼ lime or lemon, peeled
½ cup pineapple chunks (fresh or frozen)
¼ cup mango chunks (fresh or frozen)
1 tsp. flax or sesame seeds
½ cup milk (regular, coconut, almond, or soy)
4 ice cubes

Place all ingredients in a blender and blend on high until smooth. Add more milk if a thinner smoothie is desired.

Serves 1.

Cottage Cheese Pancakes

1 cup cottage cheese
4 eggs
½ cup flour
¼ tsp. salt
¼ cup oil
½ cup milk
½ tsp. vanilla

Combine all ingredients until well blended. Cook on a lightly greased griddle.

Serves 4.

Creamed Eggs on Toast

4 T. butter
4 T. flour
2 cups milk
4 to 6 hard-boiled eggs, peeled and chopped
Salt and pepper to taste
4 pieces whole wheat bread, toasted

In a medium saucepan, melt butter on medium-low heat. Gradually whisk in the flour so it doesn't become lumpy. Continue whisking the flour/butter mixture while adding the milk and then until mixture just comes to a boil and thickens.

Remove from heat and add hard-boiled eggs and salt and pepper to taste. Spoon over toast.

Serves 4.

Note: You can easily make a larger batch of creamed eggs if you're feeding a lot of people by simply doubling this recipe, but if eggs are limited, you can get away with only 6 eggs for a double batch.

Eat Your Greens Smoothie

2 handfuls fresh greens (lettuce, spinach, Swiss chard, or kale)
1 banana, peeled and chunked
½ cup seedless grapes
1 pear or apple, peeled, cored, and chunked
2 T. unsalted almonds
1 cup coconut or almond milk
4 ice cubes

Combine all ingredients in a blender and blend on high until smooth.

Serves 1 or 2.

Ham and Onion Frittata ✓

2 T. butter
½ cup onion, diced
1 cup ham, diced
8 eggs
3 T. milk
½ cup shredded cheddar or Monterey Jack cheese
Salt and pepper to taste

Preheat the oven to 350°.

In a heavy ovenproof skillet (cast iron works well), melt the butter and then add the onion and ham and sauté for about 4 minutes.

While the ham and onion are cooking, in a medium mixing bowl whisk together the eggs, milk, cheese, salt, and pepper. Pour in the hot skillet and stir to mix all ingredients.

Place the skillet into the oven and bake for about 15 to 20 minutes or until the frittata is puffed and golden and a knife inserted into the center comes out clean.

Serves 4 to 6.

Hush Puppies

4 slices bacon
1 cup stone-ground cornmeal
1 tsp. baking powder
½ tsp. salt
1 egg
½ cup milk (may need a bit more)

Fry bacon until crisp. Cool and crumble into pieces and set aside.

In a medium mixing bowl, combine the cornmeal, baking powder, and salt. Beat together the egg and milk and combine it with the dry ingredients, mixing well. Add the bacon pieces and stir again.

Deep-fry hush puppies until golden brown, turning once.

Serves 4.

"Instant" Oatmeal ✓

Note: Make this recipe ahead of time so on busy mornings, when time is at a premium, this "fast food" will still provide you and your family a healthy breakfast.

6 cups quick-cooking or old-fashioned rolled oats
⅓ cup brown sugar
2 tsp. cinnamon
¾ to 1 tsp. salt

Spread the oats on a baking sheet (you may need to do this in two batches, depending on the size of your baking sheet). Bake in a preheated 325° oven for 20 minutes. Cool.

Combine 4 cups of the oats, brown sugar, cinnamon, and salt in a food processor and pulse just until you achieve a rough powder. Mix the remaining 2 cups of oats into the pulsed oats and stir well to thoroughly combine.

Place the oatmeal in a large container with a tight-fitting lid and store in the pantry or a cupboard, where it will stay fresh for several months—no need to refrigerate.

To make the instant oatmeal:
Place ½ cup of the dry mixture in a bowl and pour in about 1 cup of boiling water (you can use a bit more if you like your oatmeal thinner). Stir and then cover the bowl with a plate. Let the oatmeal sit for about 5 minutes; stir again and serve.

You can add some warm milk (consider using less boiling water if you choose to add milk), fruit, nuts, seeds, and/or raisins to the oatmeal.

Makes 12 servings.

Kale and Banana Breakfast Smoothie

1 handful torn kale
1 banana, peeled and chunked
½ cup berries (fresh or frozen)
1 T. sunflower seed or chopped nuts
1 cup coconut milk (use more if you prefer a thinner smoothie)
4 ice cubes

Place all ingredients in a blender and blend on high speed until smooth.

Serves 1.

Note: It's easy to freeze kale or other greens. Simply rinse the leaves and let them drain. Then tear into pieces and place them on a large baking pan. Place in the freezer until completely frozen. Then transfer the frozen greens to a large freezer bag. Press down on the bag to remove as much air as possible. Seal and place back in the freezer. When ready to use, take out what you need—no need to thaw first. Kale can stay frozen for several months if care is taken to remove as much air from the bag as possible.

Oatmeal Pancakes

Note: These pancakes are started the night before.

2 cups rolled oats
2 cups buttermilk
½ cup unbleached white flour
½ cup whole wheat flour
2 tsp. sugar
1½ tsp. baking powder
1½ tsp. baking soda
1 tsp. salt
2 eggs
2 T. butter, melted and cooled slightly

In the evening, combine the oats and buttermilk in a mixing bowl. Cover and refrigerate overnight.

The next morning, in another mixing bowl, sift together the flours, sugar, baking powder, baking soda, and salt. Set aside.

In a large mixing bowl, whisk the eggs until they are light and frothy. Stir in the melted butter. Add the oatmeal-buttermilk mixture and mix well. Blend in the flour mixture. You will need to stir with a wooden spoon at this point because the mixture will be very thick. If it appears too dry, you can add a few more tablespoons of buttermilk or regular milk.

Fry the pancakes in a small amount of oil, cooking well on both sides. These pancakes really puff up as they cook.

Serve the pancakes hot from the griddle with a pat of butter if desired, but they are also excellent plain.

Serves 4 to 6.

Spinach and Veggie Crustless Breakfast Quiche

1 10-ounce box frozen spinach, thawed, rinsed, and squeezed dry
⅓ cup mushrooms, sliced
⅓ cup onion, diced
⅓ cup bell pepper, diced
1 clove garlic, minced
4 eggs
1 cup milk
Salt and pepper to taste
1 cup cheese (Gruyère, Swiss, or cheddar)
2 T. Parmesan cheese

Preheat the oven to 350°.

Lightly butter or grease a 10-inch pie pan; place the spinach in the bottom of the pan.

In a sauté pan, cook the mushrooms, onion, bell pepper, and garlic in a bit of oil or butter (or use a nonstick sauté pan) until the vegetables are softened slightly; place on top of the spinach in the pie pan.

In a medium mixing bowl, whisk together the eggs, milk, salt, and pepper; pour over the vegetables in the pie pan. Next, sprinkle the cheeses evenly across the top of the egg mixture.

Bake for 45 to 55 minutes or until the quiche is set and the top is golden brown.

Serves 6 to 8.

Note: This reheats very well in the microwave and also makes a great light lunch dish served with a green salad.

Spinach Egg Bake

4 bunches green onions, finely chopped
¼ cup butter
1 lb. fresh spinach, stems trimmed
6 T. fresh parsley, minced
12 eggs
½ cup sour cream
½ tsp. salt
1½ cups (6 ounces) shredded cheddar cheese
½ cup grated Parmesan cheese

Preheat the oven to 350°.

In a large skillet, sauté the green onions in butter for 2 minutes or until tender. Add spinach and parsley; sauté 3 minutes longer or until heated through. Remove from the heat and set aside.

In a large bowl, beat the eggs, sour cream, and salt until smooth. Stir in the spinach mixture and cheddar cheese. Pour into a buttered or greased 10 x 15-inch baking pan. Sprinkle with Parmesan cheese.

Bake uncovered for 25 to 30 minutes or until a knife inserted near the center comes out clean. Cut into squares and serve.

Serves 10 to 12.

Note: This makes a large batch, so feel free to halve the recipe for a smaller amount.

Zucchini Frittata

3 T. olive oil, divided
1 T. butter
2 cloves garlic, minced
2 cups zucchini, sliced
½ cup onion, diced
8 eggs
3 T. milk (or half-and-half)
½ tsp. oregano
½ tsp. salt
⅛ –¼ tsp. pepper
3 T. grated Parmesan cheese

In a large (10 to 12 inches) ovenproof skillet, heat 2 tablespoons of the olive oil and the butter. When the butter is melted and the mixture is hot, add the garlic, zucchini, and onion. Sauté, stirring occasionally, for about 5 minutes. Remove from heat, but keep the stove on.

In a large mixing bowl, beat the eggs and milk. Stir in the oregano, salt, pepper, and Parmesan cheese.

Turn on your oven's broiler to preheat.

Place the skillet back on the heat and drizzle the last tablespoon of oil over the vegetables. When the oil is hot, pour in the egg and cheese mixture and cook without stirring. When the eggs begin to set, lift the edges with a spatula and allow the uncooked egg to flow underneath. Continue lifting and cooking until the eggs are set and the top looks moist and creamy.

Place the skillet under the preheated broiler about 6 inches from the burner and broil for 2 or 3 minutes or until the top of the frittata looks completely cooked and has a golden color.

Cut into wedges to serve.

Serves 8.

DESSERTS

Apple Crumble Parfait

2 tsp. vanilla
3 T. maple syrup
4 cups plain yogurt
1 cup rolled oats
⅓ cup plus 1 T. almond butter
½ tsp. nutmeg
½ tsp. ground ginger
1¼ tsp. cinnamon, divided
4 tsp. coconut oil or butter
3 apples, peeled, cored, and diced

Preheat the oven to 350°.

Stir the vanilla and maple syrup into the yogurt. Cover and refrigerate until ready to use.

Combine the rolled oats, almond butter, nutmeg, ginger, and 1 teaspoon of the cinnamon. Spread the mixture onto a baking sheet and bake until golden brown but not too dark, about 10 to 15 minutes. Remove from heat and set aside to cool.

Heat the oil or butter in a frying pan on medium heat. Add the diced apples and remaining ¼ teaspoon of cinnamon. Cook until the apples are tender and golden, stirring gently but regularly, about 10 minutes. (You might have to reduce the heat so they don't become too brown.) Remove the apples and allow them to cool.

When ready to serve, spoon some of the yogurt mixture into the bottom of six parfait cups, large mugs, or glasses. Top each with some of the apple mixture and then some of the oats crumble. Repeat the layers, ending with the crumble. Serve immediately.

Serves 6.

DESSERTS

Applesauce Hand Pies

2¼ cups flour
½ tsp. salt
¾ cup shortening or lard
4 to 5 T. very cold water
1 pint no-sugar-added applesauce
1 egg white, beaten well (optional)
Cinnamon sugar to sprinkle on top (optional)

Preheat the oven to 450°.

In a mixing bowl, whisk together the flour and salt. Cut the shortening into the flour mixture using a pastry blender or two table knives until the crumbles are the size of peas.

Measure the cold water into a small cup and then pour the water onto the flour mixture a tablespoon at a time, stirring quickly with a fork. Do not overmix. The dough should look moist but not wet and form a ball that mostly comes clean from the sides of the bowl. Use the last tablespoon of water only if the dough seems too crumbly.

Gather up the dough with your hands and squeeze together to form a ball. Divide the dough into four parts and, working with one part at a time, roll the pastry out into a square about ⅛-inch thick.

Cut the square into four equal pieces. Place a few tablespoons of applesauce just off center (don't use too much) and fold the square of dough over onto itself. Crimp the edges well and carefully transfer the pie onto a baking sheet. Continue until all the dough has been used.

If you are using cinnamon sugar, brush the beaten egg white across the top of the pies and sprinkle a small amount of cinnamon sugar on top.

Bake for about 10 to 12 minutes or until the pies are flaky and golden on top.

Cool to barely warm or eat at room temperature.

Yields 16 pies.

Baked Apples with Walnuts and Raisins

4 baking apples (such as Granny Smith), cored
2 T. lemon juice
½ cup finely chopped walnuts
2 T. raisins
1 T. butter, melted and cooled slightly
2 T. brown sugar
1 tsp. cinnamon
1 cup hot water

Preheat the oven to 350°.

Peel the top third of each apple; core. Rub the exposed flesh of the apple with the lemon juice.

In a small mixing bowl, combine the walnuts, raisins, melted butter, brown sugar, and cinnamon. Place the prepared apples upright into a shallow casserole dish. Stuff the center of the apples with the walnut mixture.

Pour the hot water into the casserole dish (don't pour directly onto the apples) and bake for about 1 hour or until the apples are tender.

Remove baked apples using a slotted spoon and serve them warm.

Serves 4.

DESSERTS

DESSERTS

Baked Bananas

4 bananas
4 T. almond butter
1 tsp. cinnamon

Preheat the oven to 375°.

Peel the bananas and then cut a ½-inch-deep slit down the length of each one. Use the back of a spoon to gently widen the cut. Spread 1 tablespoon of almond butter in each banana. Sprinkle with cinnamon.

Wrap each banana in aluminum foil and bake for 15 minutes. Be careful when unwrapping the bananas because they're hot!

Serves 4.

Note: You can easily make more or fewer bananas. Simply use 1 tablespoon of almond butter per banana and then sprinkle on a pinch of cinnamon.

Bare Jam

½ lb. fresh, ripe fruit (strawberries, raspberries, peaches, blueberries, etc.)

If needed, peel and pit the fruit; cut into small pieces. Puree the fruit by whirling it in a blender or food processor or forcing it through a food mill. Or simply mash it with a potato masher as you cook it down.

Place the pureed fruit into a heavy-bottom saucepan. Turn the heat to medium and, stirring almost constantly, heat the fruit to a bare simmer. Reduce the heat and continue to cook the fruit, stirring almost constantly so the bottom doesn't scorch, until it reaches a thick, jam-like consistency.

The jam will keep in the refrigerator for about a week, so if you make more than you can use in that time, freeze the rest.

When you pull it out of the freezer to thaw, whisk the jam to re-emulsify.

Yield varies.

Note: Using this cook-down method, you can make as much or as little jam at one time as you want to.

Berries, Yogurt, and Shaved Chocolate

2 cups vanilla Greek yogurt
2 cups fresh berries, sliced if needed to make bite-sized pieces
1 dark chocolate bar, shaved (a potato peeler works well)

Gently combine the yogurt and berries. Place into individual serving bowls or goblets and sprinkle pieces of shaved chocolate on top.

Serves 8 to 12.

Berry Coulis

2 cups fresh or frozen strawberries or raspberries
½ tsp. lemon juice

If using frozen berries, remove them from the freezer and allow to thaw before making the coulis.

Using a food processor or blender, process berries and lemon juice until smooth; strain with a fine-mesh strainer to remove seeds. (This isn't absolutely necessary, but it makes for a more refined finished product.)

Cover and refrigerate as needed. Use within one week or freeze.

Coulis is excellent mixed into plain yogurt, whipped with coconut or regular milk and some ice cubes for a refreshing smoothie, or used as a topping for pancakes, waffles, panna cotta, or cottage cheese.

Berry Frozen Fruit Pops

1 cup berries (raspberries, strawberries, blackberries, blueberries, etc.)
2 cups plain yogurt
½ cup apple or orange juice

Blend the berries to a smooth texture. Add the yogurt and juice and blend to mix.

Pour into ice pop molds or use small, stiff paper cups. Pop them into the freezer. (If using paper cups, when the pops are partially frozen, insert wooden craft sticks into the ice pops and continue to freeze until hard.)

Yield varies, depending on size of pop.

Chocolate Bark

2 85% dark chocolate bars (3½ ounces per bar)
½ to ¾ cup pistachios (shelled and chopped) or slivered almonds
¼ cup raisins or other dried fruit (optional)

Break the chocolate bars into small pieces for easier melting. In a double boiler, melt the chocolate, stirring until completely melted and smooth. Remove from the heat, being careful to dry the bottom of the pot that contains the melted chocolate so no water drips onto your work surface. (I use a folded kitchen towel so I don't burn myself.) With a spatula, evenly spread the melted chocolate on a parchment paper-lined cookie sheet (alternatively, you can use a silicone baking mat on the cookie sheet instead of parchment paper). Sprinkle the dried fruit and nuts evenly over the melted chocolate and then refrigerate or freeze until the chocolate hardens. When ready to eat, remove the bark from the freezer and break into small pieces. Any leftovers can be stored in the refrigerator or freezer for several days.

Serves approximately 8 to 12, depending on serving size.

Note: The darker the chocolate, the lower the sugar content. If you usually eat milk chocolate, start by making this recipe using a 70% chocolate bar and work your way up to 85% chocolate.

Chocolate Dipped Bananas

2 large ripe bananas, peeled and cut into 6 equal slices each
12 paper lollipop sticks or wooden skewers
¾ cup dark chocolate chips
¼ cup finely chopped unsalted peanuts, almonds, or a combination

Line a baking sheet with waxed paper. Stick the lollipop sticks in the middle of each banana piece; set aside.

In a double boiler, melt the chocolate chips, stirring until completely melted and smooth. Alternatively, you can microwave the chocolate chips in 30-second intervals, stirring each time, until the chocolate is melted and smooth. (You won't use all of the melted chocolate, but the amount will mean it's easier to coat the banana pieces.)

Roll each banana piece in the melted chocolate, and then roll sparingly in the chopped nuts. Place the finished banana pops on the waxed paper with the sticks facing up, and then freeze the pops for about 30 minutes or until firm.

Serves 12 (2 pieces each).

Note: If you have leftover melted chocolate you would like to use up, you can cut another banana per the directions above and spoon the melted chocolate over the banana to coat.

DESSERTS

Chocolate Peanut Butter Cups

1 cup creamy, no-sugar-added peanut butter
1 T. coconut oil
1 T. honey
1 cup dark chocolate chips

Have a mini muffin tin ready.

Put the peanut butter, coconut oil, and honey in a microwavable bowl, and microwave on high for about 30 seconds or until melted. Stir mixture, and then divide it equally in the mini muffin cups.

Place the chocolate chips in a microwavable bowl and microwave on high for about 30 seconds or until melted. Pour melted chocolate over the peanut butter mixture. Place the muffin tin in the freezer for about an hour, and then carefully release the peanut butter cups using a knife to scrape around the edges of the cups.

Yield varies depending on size of cups. I usually get about 18 to 20 peanut butter cups.

Note: If you have paper or foil muffin cup liners that fit, the peanut butter cups will be easier to handle. But it's not absolutely necessary.

Chocolate Pudding

3 T. cornstarch
4 T. sugar
2 ounces unsweetened chocolate
⅛ tsp. salt
2 cups milk, divided
1 tsp. vanilla

In a medium, heavy-bottom saucepan, place the cornstarch, sugar, chocolate, and salt. Add ¼ cup of the milk, and stir to mix.

In another saucepan, heat the remaining milk, and then slowly add it to the cornstarch mixture, stirring constantly. Cook on medium-low heat, stirring constantly, until the mixture thickens. Reduce the heat a bit and continue to cook for another few minutes.

Remove from heat and add the vanilla. Pour into a serving bowl (or use individual bowls).

Cover and refrigerate until chilled.

Serves 4.

Chocolate Puff Triangles

½ cup cream cheese
2 T. sugar
⅓ cup (2 ounces) dark chocolate, finely chopped
2 T. unsalted almonds, chopped
20 wonton wrappers
1 egg
1 T. water

Preheat the oven to 375°.

DESSERTS

Line a large baking pan with foil that has been sprayed with cooking spray, or use a silicone baking mat.

In a mixing bowl, beat together the cream cheese and sugar until smooth. Stir in the chocolate and almond pieces.

Keep wonton wrappers covered except when filling so they don't dry out. Spoon about 1½ teaspoons of the chocolate mixture into the center of the wrapper; lightly moisten the edges of the wrapper, and then fold over to form a triangle. Press edges to seal. Place on the prepared baking pan and continue to fill and fold the remaining wonton wrappers.

In another small bowl, whisk together the egg and water. Brush egg mixture over the triangles, and bake for 12 to 14 minutes or until the wontons are golden and crisp.

Allow chocolate puffs to cool down to warm before eating.

Yields 20 chocolate puffs.

Chocolatey Oatmeal, Coconut, and Banana Cookies

1 cup rolled oats
⅓ cup (scant) ground almonds (use a blender or food processor)
1 cup unsweetened, shredded coconut
¼ tsp. cinnamon
½ tsp. baking powder
2 large ripe bananas, peeled
½ tsp. vanilla
5 T. coconut oil (warmed so it's liquid) or olive oil
½ cup chocolate chips

Preheat the oven to 350°.

Butter or grease 2 large baking sheets.

In a large mixing bowl, combine the rolled oats, ground almonds, shredded coconut, cinnamon, and baking powder.

In a smaller bowl, mash the bananas well; stir in the vanilla and oil. Add banana mixture to the dry ingredients and mix well. Stir in chocolate chips.

Drop 20 tablespoonfuls of dough onto the prepared baking sheets, 10 on each. Flatten the tops slightly so the cookies are about 1½ inches in diameter.

Bake for 15-20 minutes or until golden. Remove from the oven and let cookies sit on the baking sheets for a few minutes before transferring them to a wire rack to cool.

Yields 20 cookies.

Cream Puffs with Lightly Sweetened Whipped Cream

Cream puffs:
1 cup water
½ cup butter
1 tsp. sugar
¼ tsp. salt
1 cup flour, sifted
4 eggs

Sweetened whipped cream:
1 cup heavy cream
2 tsp. sugar or to taste
Small splash of vanilla

Preheat the oven to 425°.

For cream puffs: Heat the water, butter, sugar, and salt to a full rolling boil in a large saucepan. Add the flour all at once. Stir vigorously with a wooden spoon until mixture forms a thick, smooth ball that leaves the sides of the pan clean, about 1 minute. Remove from heat.

Add the eggs, one at a time, beating well after each addition with wooden spoon, until paste is shiny and smooth. Scoop out the dough onto a baking sheet in 10 equal portions and bake for 15 minutes. Reduce the heat to 375° and bake for 5 more minutes. Cut a slash in the lower side of each puff and continue baking for 10 minutes more or until puffs are firm, dry to the touch, and golden brown. Cool on a wire rack.

For sweetened whipped cream: Combine the heavy cream, sugar, and vanilla. Beat on high speed until the cream has thickened and soft peaks form when the beaters are lifted out.

Assembling the cream puffs: Cut tops off the cream puffs, fill with sweetened whipped cream, place tops back on top of the whipped cream, and serve.

Yields 10 cream puffs.

Dark Chocolate Dipped Strawberries

1 lb. fresh strawberries, stems attached, if possible
½ lb. 70% to 85% dark chocolate
Nuts (walnuts, almonds, or pecans), finely chopped (optional)

Wash the strawberries and place them on paper towels to dry. The berries need to be dry so the chocolate will stick to them. (I pat and turn the berries so all surfaces touch the paper towels.)

Break the chocolate into pieces and melt it in a double boiler or microwave it for 30 seconds at a time, removing the bowl from the microwave at 30-second intervals to give it a quick stir. (I think the double boiler does a better job because you can control the melt easier, but that's just my preference.) When the chocolate is mostly melted, remove from heat and stir until it is completely melted and smooth.

Line a baking sheet or flat plate with parchment or waxed paper, or use a silicon baking mat.

Grab a strawberry by the stem and dip it into the chocolate about halfway up the strawberry, swirling to make sure it's completely covered with the melted chocolate. Set the dipped strawberry on the prepared baking sheet or plate, and continue working as quickly as possible until all the berries are covered.

Allow the chocolate to set up and harden. You can place the berries in the refrigerator for about 30 minutes to help the process along.

For a special and elegant treat, immediately after dipping strawberries in the chocolate, you can dip the tips in finely chopped nuts.

Fresh Applesauce

6 cups apples, peeled, cored, and diced
1 T. lemon juice
Cinnamon or cinnamon sugar (optional)

Place the apples and lemon juice in a heavy-bottom pot and bring to a gentle simmer, stirring occasionally. Cover and cook, still stirring occasionally, for about 30 minutes or until the apples are soft and losing their shape.

Remove from heat and mash or puree the apples. You can serve the applesauce warm or refrigerate for later use. For a special treat, shake a small amount of cinnamon or cinnamon sugar on top of each serving.

Nut Balls

$^2/_3$ cup butter
1 cup ground nut meats (try walnuts, pecans, or a combination)
1 cup flour, sifted
3 T. sugar
1 tsp. vanilla
Pinch of salt
½ cup powdered sugar, more or less

Preheat the oven to 375°.

Place all ingredients except powdered sugar in a bowl and work with fingers until well blended. Shape into balls the size of large marbles and place on an ungreased baking sheet.

Bake for 10 minutes. After baking, while still warm, roll in powdered sugar.

Makes approximately 50 balls.

Old-Fashioned Baked Rice Pudding

4 cups milk
½ tsp. salt
¼ cup sugar
¼ tsp. nutmeg
3 T. uncooked long-grain white rice

Butter a high-sided 2-quart baking dish (I use a soufflé dish); add all of the ingredients and stir to mix.

Bake at 300° for about 3½ hours, stirring every 20 minutes during the first hour. (This helps to keep the rice from settling to the bottom of the baking dish.)

Serves 6 to 8.

Panna Cotta

¼ cup water
2 tsp. unflavored gelatin
2¾ cups cream
½ cup sweetened condensed milk
1 vanilla bean

In a medium mixing bowl, add the water; sprinkle the gelatin over the water and allow to sit for several minutes to soften.

In a heavy saucepan, combine the cream and condensed milk. Split the vanilla bean and scrape out the seeds into the cream mixture before adding the pod itself to the mixture. Bring mixture to a simmer over medium-high heat, stirring regularly. Turn off the heat and let the mixture sit for 15 minutes.

Remove the vanilla pod from the cream and carefully scrape again to loosen as many seeds as possible into the cream mixture.

Slowly pour the cream mixture into the mixing bowl with the gelatin and water, whisking constantly. Continue whisking until the gelatin has completely dissolved.

Pour mixture through a fine-mesh screen or colander to remove any errant bits of vanilla bean pod and then pour the panna cotta into individual serving bowls or one larger bowl.

Cover the panna cotta with plastic wrap and refrigerate for at least 4 hours. Serve plain or topped with fresh berries.

Serves 8 to 10.

Pear and Sweet Cherry Crisp

3 Medjool dates, pitted and finely chopped
½ cup nuts, chopped (pecans, walnuts, and almonds are great choices)
2 T. butter, melted (or 2 T. coconut oil, melted)
2 T. whole wheat flour
2 T. milk
1 cup rolled oats, divided
2 cups pears, cored and chopped
2 cups sweet cherries, pitted
½ tsp. ground cardamom
2 tsp. vanilla
2 T. maple syrup

Preheat the oven to 400°.

Lightly grease or butter four 8-ounce ovenproof ramekins or baking dishes.

DESSERTS

In a food processor, combine the dates, nuts, melted butter, flour, milk, and ½ cup of the rolled oats. Process until crumbly, about 1 to 2 minutes.

In a mixing bowl, gently combine the pears, cherries, cardamom, and remaining ½ cup rolled oats. Drizzle the vanilla and maple syrup over the mixture and gently mix again. Divide the fruit mixture evenly between the four prepared ramekins and sprinkle the nut topping over the fruit.

Cover the ramekins with foil and bake for 15 minutes. Remove the foil and continue baking until the fruit is bubbling and the topping is golden brown, another 10 minutes or so.

Serves 4.

Pear Cheddar Crisp

2 ripe pears, cored and thinly sliced
3 ounces cheddar cheese, thinly sliced
½ cup rolled oats
1 T. brown sugar
1 tsp. cinnamon
4 tsp. butter, melted

Preheat the oven to 400°.

Place four 8- to 10-ounce baking dishes or ramekins on a baking sheet. Divide the pear and cheese slices among the baking dishes, arranging them alternately and cutting to fit if necessary.

In a small bowl, combine the rolled oats, brown sugar, and cinnamon. Stir in the melted butter, and mix to incorporate. Sprinkle over the pear and cheese mixture.

Bake for 15 minutes or until the cheese is melted and the crisp is hot throughout.

Serves 4.

Pineapple Ice

1 can (20 ounces) crushed pineapple, juice-packed, undrained
2 cups buttermilk or plain yogurt
½ tsp. vanilla

Place the undrained pineapple in a blender or food processor and process until the fruit is pureed. Transfer the puree to a mixing bowl and add the yogurt and vanilla and stir to mix.

Put the pineapple mixture into a freezer container. Cover and freeze until firm.

To serve, pull the pineapple ice from the freezer about 30 minutes before serving; scrape with an ice-cream scoop into dessert bowls.

Serves 6 to 8.

Pumpkin Bars

½ cup (1 stick) butter
½ cup brown sugar
½ tsp. baking soda
½ tsp. pumpkin pie spice
⅓ cup canned pumpkin
1 egg
1½ cups flour
4 ounces cream cheese
1 cup frozen light whipped dessert topping, thawed
Nutmeg (optional)

Preheat the oven to 350°.

Grease and lightly flour a square baking dish.

In a mixing bowl, combine the butter, brown sugar, baking soda, and pumpkin pie spice. Beat with a mixer until well blended. Beat in the pumpkin and egg and then the flour last. Spread the batter into the prepared baking dish.

DESSERTS

Bake 12 to 15 minutes or until a toothpick inserted comes out clean. Cool in the pan for 10 minutes. Remove the cake to cool on a wire rack.

In a bowl, beat the cream cheese until it is softened and smooth. Beat in half of the whipped topping until well mixed; fold in the remaining whipped topping. Spread on top of the cooled, uncut pumpkin bars. Cut into 25 squares (5 down and 5 across) and sprinkle lightly with nutmeg if using.

Yields 25 pumpkin bars.

Ricotta Cheese with Raspberries and Walnuts

½ cup coarsely chopped walnuts
1 cup ricotta cheese
½ cup raspberries
2 tsp. honey or maple syrup
½ tsp. cinnamon

Place the walnuts in a dry frying pan and cook over medium heat until they begin to darken and smell toasted, about 4 minutes. Stir regularly to toast all sides. Remove the walnuts from the frying pan and cool.

Place the ricotta in a shallow bowl or serving plate; sprinkle the walnuts and raspberries evenly across the top of the ricotta. Drizzle the honey or maple syrup over all, and sprinkle with the cinnamon. Serve immediately.

Serves 4 to 6.

Strawberries with Coconut Cream and Dark Chocolate

For each serving:

½ to 1 cup fresh strawberries, hulled and sliced or cut into bite-sized pieces
1 to 3 tablespoons canned coconut cream, crumbled
Shaved dark chocolate (70% or higher), enough for sprinkling on top

Place the strawberries and coconut cream crumbles into a serving bowl. Mix gently. Add a small amount of shaved dark chocolate on top.

Note: Canned coconut cream can be hard to find, but canned coconut milk works just as well. Make sure that the coconut milk has no ingredients other than coconut meat, water, and possibly guar gum. Don't buy the light varieties, and if your budget allows, select organic. When you open the can, you'll see that the cream has risen to the top (it looks like ricotta cheese or yogurt), and this is what you want to use. If you don't use the entire can (and you won't), place the leftover cream or milk in a container with a tight-fitting lid and store in the refrigerator. Use within several days for another recipe. (It tastes great with cooked oatmeal, cereal, smoothies, iced coffee, salad dressing, or cream soups. If you bought coconut milk, remember that the cream and milk have separated, so be sure to stir them together before adding to a recipe.)

Vanilla Pudding

3 T. cornstarch
4 T. sugar
⅛ tsp. salt
2 cups milk, divided
1 tsp. vanilla

In a medium, heavy-bottom saucepan, mix the cornstarch, sugar, and salt. Add ¼ cup of the milk and stir to mix.

In another saucepan, heat the remaining milk, and then slowly add it to the cornstarch mixture, stirring constantly. Cook on medium-low heat, stirring constantly, until the mixture thickens. Reduce the heat a bit and continue to cook for another few minutes.

Remove from heat and add the vanilla. Pour into a serving bowl (or use individual bowls), cover, and refrigerate until chilled.

Serves 4.

Whipped Mocha Cream

3 cups ricotta cheese
3 T. finely ground coffee beans
4 T. sugar
¾ tsp. cinnamon
Dash of nutmeg
3 tsp. vanilla
2 T. unsweetened cocoa powder

In a mixing bowl, whisk together all of the ingredients. Cover and refrigerate for at least two hours so the coffee grounds soften and the flavors meld.

When ready to serve, place in stemmed goblets or dessert bowls. You can also shave a small amount of dark chocolate on top of each serving, which will make it special enough for company!

Serves 8.

GRAINS AND NOODLES

Amaranth

1 cup amaranth
2½ cups water or broth
Pinch of salt (if using water)

Soak the amaranth in cold water for two hours or overnight. (If overnight, place in the fridge.) When ready to cook, drain with a fine mesh strainer.

In a medium saucepot, combine the amaranth, 2½ cups fresh water or broth, and a pinch of salt if using water. Bring to a boil, reduce the heat, cover the pot, and simmer for 20 minutes, stirring occasionally so the bottom doesn't burn. Lift the lid to see if the amaranth looks tripled in size and is fluffy. If not, cover the pot and let it simmer for another few minutes.

Note: You can make amaranth cereal by boiling 1 cup amaranth in 3 cups water for 30 minutes. Serve warm, with milk and a bit of cinnamon or honey.

Barley

Note: You can buy hulled barley, which has only had the inedible hull removed. Pearled barley (also called pearl or pot barley) has been polished to remove the bran. Hulled barley is chewier and takes longer to cook, while pearled barley takes less time to cook and has a more refined taste and texture.

1 part pearled or hulled barley
3 parts water or broth
Salt

To cook either kind of barley, bring the amount of liquid you need to a boil—for instance, 3 cups liquid if you are going to cook 1 cup barley. Add the barley and a pinch or two of salt if desired and simmer on low heat, covered, for at least 45 minutes for pearled, and about twice that for hulled.

GRAINS AND
NOODLES

71

You can freeze cooked, cooled barley. Simply thaw it before using. Or throw it in a soup pot toward the end of the cooking with the other ingredients to thaw quickly and heat through.

Barley and Pine Nut Pilaf

1 cup pearled barley
3⅓ cups chicken broth
6 T. butter
⅓ cup (2 ounces) pine nuts
1 cup green onions
½ cup fresh parsley (or 2½ T. dried)
¼ tsp. salt
¼ tsp. pepper

Preheat the oven to 350°.

Rinse the barley in cold water and drain.

In a medium stockpot, heat the chicken broth and bring it to a boil.

While the broth is heating, in a 2 to 2½-quart ovenproof, heavy-bottom pot, melt the butter. Add the pine nuts and brown them, stirring, until they are lightly toasted and golden. Remove the pine nuts with a slotted spoon and set aside. Add the green onions and barley to the pot; sauté for several minutes and then remove the barley mixture from the heat but keep it in the pot. Stir in the pine nuts, parsley, salt, and pepper and stir. Pour the boiling broth over the barley mixture and bake uncovered in the oven for 1 hour and 10 minutes. Check the pilaf at 50 minutes and add a small amount of boiling broth or water if it seems too dry.

Serves 6.

Barley and Wild Rice Pilaf

2 T. butter
½ cup pearled barley
½ cup onion, chopped
1 clove garlic, minced
1 can (14½ ounces) chicken broth
1 cup water
½ cup wild rice, rinsed and drained
½ tsp. grated lemon peel
¼ tsp. pepper, to taste

In a medium, heavy-bottom pot, melt the butter over medium heat. Add the barley and cook for 6 to 8 minutes, stirring regularly, until lightly browned. Add the onion and garlic and cook, stirring for 2 to 3 minutes more.

Add the broth and water and then raise the heat slightly to bring the liquid to a boil. Stir in the wild rice, lemon peel, and pepper; return to a boil. Reduce the heat to low, cover, and simmer for about an hour or until the barley and rice are tender. (I usually start checking at about 50 minutes.)

Serves 4 to 6.

GRAINS AND
NOODLES

Barley Casserole

3 T. butter plus ½ cup (1 stick) butter, divided
½ lb. mushrooms
2 medium onions, diced
1½ cups pearled barley
3 cups chicken or beef broth (approximately), divided
Salt and pepper to taste
Fresh parsley for garnish, chopped

Melt 3 tablespoons butter in a heavy skillet and then add the mushrooms. Sauté over medium heat for 4 minutes. Transfer the mushrooms to a small dish and set aside.

Add the butter to the skillet and heat on medium until it melts. Add the onions and cook until they are just wilted. Add the barley and stir constantly over medium-high heat until the barley has a rich golden color. (Be careful not to burn.) Remove the skillet from the heat.

Stir in the mushrooms and then pour the mixture into a buttered or oiled 1½-quart casserole or baking dish.

Heat the broth and add about 1½ cups to the barley mixture. Cover the casserole dish and place in a preheated 350° oven for 30 minutes. Remove the cover and add another 1½ cups broth to the barley mixture. Cover again and bake another 30 minutes.

Add salt and pepper to the casserole. Add more broth if the barley has absorbed too much liquid before it is tender.

Right before serving, sprinkle with parsley.

Serves 4 to 6.

Brown Rice to Freeze

Note: Brown rice takes much longer to cook than its processed cousin, so it just makes sense to cook a large batch of medium- or

*long-grain brown rice ahead of time and then freeze in meal-sized
portions for later use. For every 1 cup of uncooked brown rice, you
will need 2½ cups water or broth. One cup of raw rice will equal
about 3 cups cooked.*

*You may want to soak the uncooked brown rice for an hour if you
prefer softer cooked rice. (Young children might be more willing to
eat it this way, so give it a try if you have reluctant eaters.) Drain the
rice and discard the soaking liquid.*

> 1 part brown rice
> 2½ parts water or broth

In a large pot, add the rice and fresh water or broth according
to the ratios listed above. Bring to a boil. Cover and reduce the
heat to low. Keep the rice mixture barely simmering until done,
about 45 to 60 minutes. You can begin checking the rice to see
if it's done after about 30 minutes. When done, remove the pot
from the heat and, keeping the lid on, let the rice sit for about 5
minutes before serving.

If freezing, uncover the pot and fluff the rice; let it sit for about
30 minutes to help it cool down. Place serving-sized portions
into freezer bags or containers and place in freezer until needed.

Bulgur

> 1 cup bulgur
> 2 cups water
> ½ tsp. salt

Combine the bulgur, water, and salt in a saucepan. Bring to a
boil and then reduce the heat, cover the pot, and simmer for 15
minutes or until tender.

Note: *While you can buy bulgur in the bulk foods section at many
grocery stores, it's also sold prepackaged, so feel free to follow the package directions instead.*

GRAINS AND NOODLES

Farro

1 cup farro
3 cups water or broth

Rinse and drain the farro. Place the farro in a pot and add enough water or broth to cover (about 3 cups will be plenty). Bring to a boil and then reduce the heat, cover the pot, and simmer for about 30 minutes. When the farro is to your liking (try a few kernels), drain off excess water.

Note: Farro is a nutritious stand-in for rice or porridge, added to soups, stews, and curries, or chilled and mixed with veggies and salad dressing for a tasty, hearty salad.

Millet Pilaf

2 cups millet
2 T. curry powder
4 cups chicken or vegetable broth (might need a bit more)
2 T. butter
½ cup zucchini, diced or shredded
½ cup yellow summer squash, diced or shredded (or use all zucchini—1 cup total)
¼ cup bell pepper, minced (any color)
¼ cup green onions, chopped
¼ cup tomatoes, diced
Salt and pepper to taste

Toast the millet in a large saucepan over low heat, stirring constantly until the grains turn light brown (this will probably take less than a minute). Remove from heat and stir in the curry powder. Cool for 5 minutes.

Return the millet to the stove and add the broth. Bring to a boil and then reduce the heat, cover, and simmer for about 25 minutes. Check at about 20 minutes to make sure there is still a bit of liquid in the saucepan. If not, add a very small amount of broth so it doesn't boil dry.

While the millet is cooking, melt the butter in a skillet and sauté the zucchini, summer squash, bell pepper, and green onions on low heat, stirring occasionally. Turn off the heat and add the tomatoes. When the millet is done, pour in the vegetables and stir gently to combine. Salt and pepper to taste and serve hot.

Quinoa

1 part quinoa
2 parts water or broth

Rinse the quinoa well and then drain.

Combine quinoa and water or broth. Bring to a boil and then reduce the heat, cover, and cook for 15 minutes. Cool for 5 minutes and then fluff with a fork.

Note: You can use quinoa hot as a side dish (add your favorite spices), or allow it to cool completely and make a tasty salad by adding chopped fresh vegetables and salad dressing of your choice.

Spaghetti Squash Noodles

1 spaghetti squash
2 T. olive oil
Salt and pepper

Preheat the oven to 375°.

Cut the spaghetti squash lengthwise in half; scoop out seeds. Drizzle each half with 1 tablespoon of olive oil and then sprinkle on salt and pepper.

GRAINS AND
NOODLES

Place the squash, cut side down, on a baking sheet and bake for about 45 to 60 minutes, depending on the size of the squash.

When cooked, use two forks to scoop out and separate the squash strands and use in place of noodles in any recipe, or liberally butter the squash strands, sprinkle on more salt and pepper to taste, and eat as is. You can also be creative. Besides butter, salt, and pepper, try adding Parmesan cheese, herbs and spices, and garlic in any combination that suits you.

Whole Wheat Egg Noodles

1½ cups whole wheat flour (Durham wheat is the best variety for noodles, but any whole wheat flour will work.)
1 tsp. salt
3 large eggs
1 T. olive oil

In a mixing bowl or on a clean kitchen counter (saves washing the bowl!), combine the flour and salt. Make a well in the middle of the flour mixture and add the eggs and oil into the well. Using a fork, whisk the eggs and oil and then slowly begin to incorporate the flour.

Once the dough starts to form, switch to your hands and knead until the dough is smooth and not sticky, but not too stiff. Form into a flattened ball and cover the dough with a slightly damp towel; let rest for 20 minutes.

Divide the dough into eight pieces. Working with one piece at a time, roll the dough into a thin rectangle or square on a lightly floured surface and cut into strips about ¼ inch wide. (The noodles are easier to work with if they aren't too long, so I will often cut the noodles in half to shorten them.)

To cook the noodles: Bring a large pot of salted water to boiling and then add the noodles. Cook the noodles about 4 to 5 minutes depending on thickness. Drain noodles and toss them with butter, olive oil, or use in a recipe.

GRAINS AND
NOODLES

Whole Wheat Pasta Noodles (Eggless)

1½ cups whole wheat flour
½ cup warm water

Put the flour in a bowl and make a well in the center. Pour the water in the well and begin to mix using a wooden spoon.

Switch to your knuckles and knead the dough until the ball sticks together easily and isn't sticky. Add very small amounts of flour or water as needed while kneading, about 2 or 3 minutes.

Cover the bowl with plastic wrap and let the dough rest for 20 minutes.

Tear off about a third of a cup of dough and place it on a floured work surface. Roll out the dough into a thin rectangle, checking to see that it's not sticking to the work surface while you roll. Add a bit of flour to the work surface only if necessary.

Use a pizza cutter or knife to slice the dough into noodles. Pile the cut pasta loosely in a bowl or on a kitchen towel and continue rolling and cutting the remaining dough.

Bring a pot of salted water to a boil, and then drop the noodles into the boiling water. Cook until done—the time will vary depending on the thickness of the noodles, but check after 5 minutes, and then continue checking every minute until done. Drain with a colander.

Note: You can use this dough for noodles for spaghetti or cut them in wide pieces and use them for lasagna. You can even eat them plain with butter or cook them in a pot of soup.

GRAINS AND NOODLES

Wild Rice

1 cup wild rice
4 cups water or broth

Rinse the rice under cold, running water for a minute and use your fingers to gently move the kernels around to make sure the rinsing is thorough.

Place the wild rice in a pot with the water or broth; bring to a boil and then cover the pot, lower the heat, and simmer gently for about an hour. You can check to see if it's done about 45 to 50 minutes into the cooking time, but it usually takes a bit longer. You'll know the rice is done when the kernels burst open and are tender.

Note: Wild rice makes a tasty side dish when cooked with broth. But I love to keep small portions of cooked wild rice in the freezer so I have some handy to add to soups and stews. Cooked and cooled wild rice can be used in salads, or you can add cooked chicken or turkey and fresh fruit and vegetables (apples, onions, tomatoes, celery, bell peppers, etc.) mixed with a bit of mayonnaise for a filling side dish or lunch.

Zoodles (Zucchini Noodles)

6 zucchinis
2 tsp. salt

Cut the zucchinis lengthwise into thin, noodle-like shapes. Or use a vegetable peeler (or one of those nifty vegetable noodle maker tools). Sprinkle the zucchini pieces with the salt and place in a colander to drain for 30 minutes.

In a pot that is large enough to easily accommodate the zucchini, boil enough water so that the zucchini will be covered. When the water is boiling, put the zucchini strips into the pot and boil for one minute. Drain the zucchini noodles and quickly rinse with a bit of cold tap water so they cool down slightly and stop cooking.

Note: Use zoodles anywhere that noodles are called for. We especially like these with marinara sauce or buttered with Italian herbs, a small amount of diced onion and fresh tomatoes, and a clove or two of minced garlic.

GRAINS AND
NOODLES

LUNCHES AND LIGHT FARE

Cheesy Eggplant Pie

4 cups eggplant, cubed
1 onion, chopped
2 cloves garlic, minced
1 T. oil
1 tsp. oregano (or use 1 T. fresh)
1 tsp. basil (or use 1 T. fresh)
Salt and pepper to taste
1 zucchini, sliced
1½ cups mozzarella cheese, shredded
²/₃ cup evaporated milk
1 egg, beaten

Preheat the oven to 375°.

In a large frying pan, sauté the eggplant, onion, and garlic in the oil for 2 minutes, gently stirring to coat the pieces. Cover and cook until the eggplant mixture is soft, about 5 minutes, stirring occasionally. Remove from the heat and stir in the oregano, basil, salt, and pepper.

Butter the bottom and sides of a 10-inch pie pan or square baking dish. Line the bottom and sides of the pan with the zucchini slices; spoon the eggplant mixture evenly on top.

Combine the cheese, evaporated milk, and egg and then pour it over the vegetables.

Bake for 30 minutes or until the cheese is bubbly and the top is golden in spots.

Serves 6 to 8.

LUNCHES AND LIGHT FARE

Crab Quiche

1 piecrust
2 T. onion, minced
3 T. butter
1 cup crabmeat
½ tsp. salt, divided
¼ tsp. pepper, divided
3 eggs
1 cup heavy cream
1 T. tomato paste
¼ cup Gruyère or Swiss cheese, shredded

Partially bake the piecrust in a preheated 400° oven for 8 to 10 minutes.

Sauté onion in butter for 5 minutes. Add the crab, ¼ teaspoon salt, and ⅛ teaspoon pepper. Simmer for a few minute and then allow to cool slightly.

In a mixing bowl, combine the eggs, whipping cream, tomato paste, ¼ tsp. salt, and ⅛ teaspoon pepper. Add crab mixture and stir.

Pour into partially cooked pastry shell, sprinkle with cheese, and bake in the upper third of the oven at 375° for 25 to 30 minutes.

Serves 6 to 8.

LUNCHES AND LIGHT FARE

Crustless Bacon and Ham Quiche

5 slices bacon, fried and crumbled (reserve fat)
1 cup cooked ham, diced
1 cup Swiss cheese, cubed
1 cup half-and-half
3 eggs, lightly beaten
1 T. cold butter, finely diced
½ cup flour
¼ tsp. salt
¼ tsp. nutmeg
⅛ tsp. pepper
1 small bottle cap club soda (about 1 T.)

Coat a quiche dish with a small amount of the reserved bacon fat (discard remainder).

Combine all ingredients and mix well. Pour into the prepared quiche dish. Let set at room temperature for 1 hour.

Bake in a preheated 500° oven for 15 minutes. Reduce temperature to 350° and bake 10 minutes longer or until top is golden brown.

Cut into wedges or squares and serve. Also good at room temperature.

Serves 6.

Crustless Zucchini Quiche

2 cups coarsely shredded zucchini
½ cup onion, diced
4 eggs, beaten
1½ cups milk or half-and-half
1 T. flour
¼ tsp. salt
⅛ tsp. pepper
⅛ tsp. nutmeg
1½ cups Monterey Jack or Gruyère cheese, shredded
½ cup mushrooms, sliced

In a covered saucepan, cook zucchini and onion in a small amount of boiling water for 5 minutes. Drain well—press out excess liquid.

In a large mixing bowl, combine the eggs, milk, flour, salt, pepper, and nutmeg. Gently stir in the cheese, mushrooms, and zucchini mixture. Pour into an ungreased casserole dish.

Place the casserole in a large baking dish and add boiling water to surround the casserole dish to a depth of an inch.

Bake at 325° for 1 hour or until a knife inserted just off center comes out clean. Let stand for 10 minutes before serving.

Serves 6 to 8.

Dijon Veggie Frittata

1 T. butter
1 cup broccoli florets
¾ cup mushrooms, sliced
2 green onions, finely chopped
1 cup cooked ham, diced
8 eggs
¼ cup water
½ cup Dijon mustard
½ tsp. Italian seasoning
¼ tsp. garlic powder
¼ tsp. salt
Pinch of pepper
1½ cups cheddar cheese, shredded
½ cup tomatoes, chopped

Preheat the oven to 375°.

In a large frying pan, melt the butter. Add the broccoli, mushrooms, and green onions and cook until tender. Add the ham and heat through. Remove from the heat and keep the mixture warm. (I usually move the frying pan to a cold part of the stove and put a lid on.)

In a large mixing bowl, beat the eggs, water, Dijon mustard, Italian seasoning, garlic powder, salt, and pepper until well blended and foamy. Stir in the cheese, tomatoes, and ham mixture.

Pour into a shallow buttered casserole dish and bake for about 25 minutes or until a fork inserted in the center comes out clean.

Serves 6 to 8.

LUNCHES AND
LIGHT FARE

Fish Sticks with Lemon Dill Dipping Sauce

For the fish sticks:
1 egg
½ tsp. water
1 cup panko bread crumbs
2 T. fresh parsley (or 2 tsp. dried)
2 T. Parmesan cheese, grated
¼ tsp. salt
¼ tsp. pepper
1 lb. fish fillets (salmon, halibut, sole, tilapia, etc.), cut into half-inch strips

For the dipping sauce:
¾ cup mayonnaise
¼ cup plain yogurt
1½ T. lemon juice (equivalent to about half of a lemon)
½ tsp. dill weed (or use 1 tsp. fresh dill)
Pinch of salt and pepper (optional)

To make the fish sticks: Preheat the oven to 400°.

Line a baking sheet with a silicone baking mat or parchment that has been sprayed with cooking oil.

In a medium bowl, whisk together the egg with ½ teaspoon water until well blended and frothy.

In another bowl, stir together the bread crumbs, parsley, Parmesan cheese, salt, and pepper.

One at a time, dip the fish sticks into the egg mixture and then into the bread-crumb mixture, making sure to coat the fish completely. Place the fish sticks on the prepared baking sheet and bake for about 20 minutes or until the fish is cooked through and flakey.

To make the dipping sauce: In a small bowl, whisk together the mayonnaise, yogurt, lemon juice, dill weed, and salt and pepper if using.

Serves 3 to 4.

Fish Tacos

For the sauce:
¼ cup plain yogurt
¼ cup mayonnaise
1½ T. lime juice
¼ tsp. ground cumin
¼ tsp. dried oregano
¼ tsp. dried dill weed

For the fish:
4 tsp. chili powder
2 tsp. ground cumin
¼ tsp. ground red or cayenne pepper (optional)
1½ lbs. white fish fillets, such as tilapia, rockfish, or cod, cut into 1-inch
    pieces
8 corn tortillas
2 cups cabbage, thinly sliced or shredded
fresh cilantro, diced onion, diced tomatoes, and/or sliced avocado for
    garnish (optional)

To make the sauce: In a small bowl, whisk together the sauce ingredients and set aside.

To make the fish: In another small bowl, combine the chili powder, cumin, and red pepper. Lightly coat the pieces of fish with the seasoning mixture and cook them over medium heat in oil until lightly browned on all sides, about 1 minute per side. Place on paper towels to drain. Sprinkle with salt and keep warm.

To warm the tortillas: Loosely wrap the tortillas in a damp cloth towel and microwave for 30 to 45 seconds.

To assemble the tacos: Fill each tortilla with ¼ cup cabbage, a portion of fish, and 1 tablespoon of the sauce. Top with any garnishes you choose and serve immediately.

Serves 4 to 8.

LUNCHES AND LIGHT FARE

Fish Tostados

1½ lbs. white fish, such as halibut, sole, tilapia, or cod
5 T. lime juice, divided
1½ tsp. salt, divided
¼ tsp. pepper
Oil for frying
6 corn tortillas
1 cup plain yogurt
Pinch of chili powder
1 to 2 avocados
3 cups cabbage, finely shredded
¼ cup fresh cilantro, minced
Salsa (optional)

Rinse the fish and place on a plate or in a baking dish and pour 4 tablespoons of the lime juice over it; sprinkle the fish with 1 teaspoon of the salt and the pepper. Cover and refrigerate for about 20 minutes.

Meanwhile, pour about a half-inch of oil into a saucepan and heat to just under the boiling point (the oil will look rippled on the surface). Fry the tortillas one at a time until crisp, about 2 minutes total depending on how hot the oil is (watch them carefully). Place them on a plate with paper towels between them to drain. Discard most of the oil.

In a small bowl, whisk together the yogurt, chili powder, 1 tablespoon of the lime juice, and ½ teaspoon salt.

Set the saucepan you used to fry the tortillas back onto the heat and, when hot, add the fish to the pan along with the lime juice marinade. Cover and cook the fish until it's cooked and flakes easily, about 8 to 12 minutes depending on the fish and thickness. Flake the fish into small pieces.

Right before serving, pit, peel, and cube the avocados.

To assemble the tostadas, place the tortillas on individual serving plates and layer equally as follows: cabbage, flaked fish along with the juices, yogurt sauce, avocado slices, cilantro, and salsa if using. Serve immediately.

Serves 6.

Herbed Veggie Dip

½ cup mayonnaise
½ cup plain yogurt
½ tsp. salt
1 tsp. dill weed
1 tsp. parsley
1 tsp. chives, minced
1 tsp. lemon juice
1 tsp. celery seed
½ tsp. garlic powder
½ tsp. paprika

In a bowl, combine the mayonnaise and yogurt. Add the remainder of the ingredients and mix again until well combined. Chill for at least an hour.

Serve with raw vegetables (carrots, celery, cauliflower, broccoli, cherry tomatoes, bell peppers, kale chips, etc.).

Yield 1 cup.

Kale Chips

1 head curly kale
1 to 2 T. olive oil
1 tsp. salt or to taste
2 T. Parmesan cheese, grated

Wash the kale and dry thoroughly. Remove the central stems and then tear leaves into pieces, keeping in mind that they shrivel up when baked, so don't make the pieces too small. (I usually try to keep the pieces at least two to three inches on all sides.)

Place the kale in a large bowl and drizzle the olive oil over the leaves. Add the salt and then, using your hands, gently toss and massage the kale leaves to coat with the oil.

Place the kale on a baking sheet in a single layer—you may need two baking sheets to hold it all. Bake the chips in a preheated 350° oven for 10 to 15 minutes, or until the kale is just turning brown. Remove from the oven and turn off the heat. Sprinkle the Parmesan cheese over the chips and return to the still-hot oven for a minute or two to help the cheese melt a bit and adhere to the chips. Allow the kale chips to cool on the pans for several minutes before removing and eating.

When I'm making these chips, I use an entire bunch of kale and guesstimate the amounts of oil, salt, and Parmesan cheese I need to use. Just go light on the olive oil because it's easy to add too much.

Yields vary depending on amount of kale used, but you can expect a medium to large mixing bowl full.

Lamb Gyros

> 4 whole wheat pita bread rounds, cut in half
> ½ cup cucumber, peeled, seeded, and chopped
> ⅓ cup plain yogurt
> 2 T. fresh dill (or 2 tsp. dried dill weed)
> 1 tsp. oil
> ¾ lb. boneless lamb, cut into bite-sized pieces
> 2 cloves garlic, minced
> Salt and pepper to taste
> ¼ cup thinly sliced onion
> 1 tomato, chopped
> ½ cup torn spinach leaves

Wrap pitas in aluminum foil; heat at 400° until warm, about 10 minutes.

In a small bowl, combine the cucumber, yogurt, and dill weed.

In a sauté pan, add the oil, lamb, garlic, salt, and pepper and cook on medium-high heat for about 5 minutes or until meat is cooked and browned, stirring often.

To assemble the gyros: Place some of the meat, onion, tomato pieces, and spinach leaves into the pita pocket. Top with cucumber sauce and serve immediately.

Yields 8 gyros.

Meat-Filled Picnic Rolls

12 whole wheat dinner rolls or hamburger buns
¾ lb. ground beef
¾ lb. bulk pork sausage or ground pork
1 small onion, diced
1 large or 2 small cloves garlic, minced
1 small green pepper, diced
2 eggs, beaten
⅓ cup spicy prepared mustard
1 T. Worcestershire sauce
½ tsp. basil
½ tsp. oregano
½ tsp. thyme
Salt and pepper to taste
2 T. melted butter

Preheat the oven to 400°.

Split the dinner rolls (hamburger buns are already split) and pull out the centers of both the tops and bottoms, leaving ¼-inch thick crust and reserving 1 cup for the meat filling.

Crumble the ground beef and sausage into a large frying pan and cook, stirring to break up the meat until it is browned.

Add the onion, garlic, and green pepper and cook, stirring until the onion is limp. Drain off excess fat and then stir in the reserved pieces of bread, eggs, mustard, Worcestershire sauce, basil, oregano, thyme, and salt and pepper.

LUNCHES AND LIGHT FARE

Pack the meat filling into rolls or buns and brush the tops of the sandwiches with the melted butter. Bake for 15 minutes or until the rolls or buns are golden brown.

These can be eaten right away, or you can wrap the sandwiches in several layers of aluminum foil and newspaper, and they will keep warm for up to an hour.

Makes 8 to 12 sandwiches depending on size of rolls.

Note: *There is a good lesson here: If you're craving a hamburger, simply pull out the centers of the buns so you have a smaller serving of the carbohydrate-laden bread.*

Mushroom Soufflé

6 eggs
½ cup (stick) butter, plus 1 to 2 T. more for preparing soufflé dish, divided
1 T. Parmesan cheese, grated
1½ cups mushrooms, chopped
½ cup onion, chopped
1 tsp. thyme
6 T. flour
1½ tsp. salt, divided
Dash cayenne pepper
1 cup milk
½ cup Swiss or Gruyère cheese, shredded
¼ tsp. cream of tartar

Separate the eggs, placing the whites and yolks in separate large bowls. Let the whites warm to room temperature, about 1 hour.

Meanwhile, butter a 1½-quart soufflé dish. Dust with the Parmesan cheese. Wrap buttered waxed paper around the top for a 2-inch extension. Secure with kitchen string or buttered freezer tape.

Preheat the oven to 350°.

Sauté mushrooms and onion in 2 tablespoons melted butter, stirring, for 5 minutes. Stir in thyme and set aside.

Melt 5 tablespoons butter in a medium saucepan; remove from heat. Stir in the flour, ½ teaspoon of the salt, and cayenne pepper until smooth. Gradually stir in the milk. Bring to boiling over medium heat, stirring constantly until mixture becomes thick and begins to leave the bottom and sides of the saucepan.

With a wire whisk or wooden spoon, beat the egg yolks. Gradually beat in the flour mixture, Gruyère cheese, and mushroom mixture. Beat until well combined.

Add the cream of tartar and remaining ½ teaspoon of the salt to the egg whites. With clean beaters, beat until stiff peaks form when the beater is raised.

With a wire whisk or rubber spatula, fold one-third of the beaten egg whites into the warm cheese and mushroom mixture until well combined. Carefully fold in remaining egg whites until just combined. Turn the soufflé mixture into the prepared dish.

Bake for 40 minutes or until the soufflé is puffed and golden brown. Remove the collar and serve immediately.

Serves 6.

LUNCHES AND LIGHT FARE

Mushroom Turnovers

1 whole wheat, double piecrust
½ cup butter, softened
2 T. butter
½ cup onion, diced
¼ lb. fresh mushrooms, chopped
1 tsp. flour
½ tsp. garlic salt
¼ tsp. thyme
Dash black or cayenne pepper
1 egg yolk

Shape the piecrust into a ball and then roll out onto a floured work surface to a 12 x 16-inch rectangle. Spread with the softened butter to within a half inch from the edges.

Fold lengthwise into thirds, pressing edges together to seal. Then, starting at one short end, fold dough into thirds. Wrap tightly in waxed paper or plastic wrap and refrigerate at least one hour. Butter should be firm.

In a large pan, melt the 2 tablespoons butter and sauté the onion until tender and golden. Add the mushrooms and sauté another 3 to 4 minutes; remove from heat. Stir in the flour, garlic salt, thyme, and pepper and cook, stirring for 1 minute or until mixture thickens slightly. Place mixture in a medium bowl. Cover and refrigerate for at least 1 hour.

Preheat the oven to 400°.

Divide pastry in half (to make working the dough easier) and roll out each half. Cut dough using a 2½-inch biscuit or cookie cutter, making 16 rounds for each half—32 rounds in total.

Place 1 teaspoon of filling just off center of each round. Fold the dough in half over the filling and press the edges with a fork to seal. Place the turnovers on an ungreased cookie sheet.

Beat the egg yolk with 1 tablespoon water until well mixed and smooth and then brush the egg yolk mixture on each turnover.

Bake the turnovers for 15 to 20 minutes or until golden brown.

Yield 32 turnovers.

Poached Fish with Tomato Mushroom Sauce

For the fish:

1 cup water

¼ tsp. salt

1 T. lemon juice

1 lb. white fish fillets, such as sole, flounder, or halibut (fresh or frozen and thawed)

For the sauce:

2 T. butter

¼ cup onion, chopped

2 tomatoes, peeled and coarsely diced

½ cup mushrooms, sliced

¼ tsp. salt

Dash cayenne pepper

To prepare the fish: In a large skillet, combine the water, salt, and lemon juice; bring to a boil and then add the fish. Reduce the heat, cover, and simmer for 5 to 10 minutes or until the fish flakes easily with a fork.

To prepare the sauce: Meanwhile, melt the butter in a medium saucepan. Add the onion and cook, stirring, until tender. Stir in all remaining sauce ingredients and continue to cook, stirring occasionally, for 5 minutes more.

To serve, using a slotted spoon, carefully lift the fish to the serving plates and then spoon the sauce over the fish.

Serves 3 to 4.

LUNCHES AND LIGHT FARE

Notes:

Quiche Lorraine

2 cups bacon, chopped
¾ cup onion, diced
1 pastry shell, unbaked
1½ cups Swiss or Gruyère cheese, shredded
5 eggs
1½ cups milk
½ tsp. pepper
Salt to taste
Dash of nutmeg

Preheat the oven to 375°.

In a large skillet, fry the bacon until just crisp. Remove the bacon and drain on several layers of paper towels. Add the onion to the skillet and sauté until softened and beginning to become translucent, about 3 to 4 minutes.

Place the pastry shell on a large baking sheet, and then spread 1 cup of the cheese on the bottom of the pastry. Top with bacon, onion, and remaining cheese.

In a mixing bowl, whisk together the eggs, milk, pepper, and salt. Pour over the bacon mixture in the pastry shell; sprinkle with nutmeg.

Carefully place the quiche into the oven and bake for 40 to 50 minutes or until the quiche is golden brown and a knife inserted into the center comes out clean.

Serves 6.

LUNCHES AND LIGHT FARE

Salmon Pâté

1 package (8 ounces) cream cheese
3 T. grated onion
½ tsp. prepared horseradish
¼ tsp. cayenne pepper
1 can (15 ½ ounces) pink salmon, skin and bones removed and drained

Beat the cream cheese until smooth. Add the remaining ingredients and mix until well blended.

Cover and chill the pâté for at least an hour before serving. This pâté is excellent with raw veggies, crackers, or pita bread.

Yield about 2½ cups.

Spinach Timbales

2 lbs. fresh spinach
3 eggs, slightly beaten
1 cup milk
1 tsp. salt
¼ tsp. pepper
2 tsp. vinegar
1 tsp. grated onion

Preheat the oven to 350°.

Cook the spinach in a small amount of boiling water for 3 minutes. Drain well and then chop fine.

In a mixing bowl, combine the spinach and remaining ingredients. Pour the mixture into 8 individual custard cups that have been buttered or greased.

Set the custard cups (the actual number will vary depending on the size of your cups) in a large casserole dish and place in the oven. Pour boiling water into the casserole dish so the custard

LUNCHES AND
LIGHT FARE

cups have water about a third to half-way up their sides. Bake for 25 to 30 minutes or until set.

These are good alone, or you can serve them with a cheese sauce poured over them.

Serves 8.

Spinach with Noodles and Sour Cream

1¼ lbs. spinach
2 T. butter
1 onion, chopped
Small pinch nutmeg
4 ounces fettucine noodles
1 cup sour cream
2 large eggs, well beaten
1 ounce sliced almonds
Salt and pepper to taste

Preheat the oven to 375°.

Cook the spinach in a small amount of water for about 5 minutes. Drain, squeeze dry, and chop.

Melt the butter in a saucepan. Add the onion and nutmeg and sauté until onion is tender, about 4 minutes. Add to the spinach.

Cook noodles according to the package directions just until al dente; drain. Mix the noodles with the spinach mixture and gently blend.

In a small mixing bowl, whisk together the sour cream and beaten eggs until well blended; pour into the noodles and spinach mixture and gently fold to mix.

Place in a lightly buttered or oiled casserole dish, top with the almonds, and bake for 25 to 30 minutes.

Serves 6.

Summer Squash Patties

3 cups zucchini or other summer squash, grated
½ tsp. salt
3 T. fresh parsley, minced, or 1 tsp. dried
½ tsp. garlic powder
¾ cup Parmesan cheese, grated
1 egg
¾ to 1 cup flour
½ tsp. baking powder
Pinch of pepper
Oil for frying

Combine all of the ingredients except for the oil and mix well. Go easy on the flour and only use as much as needed to make a thin batter.

Pour enough oil to thoroughly coat bottom of the skillet you plan to use. Heat the oil and then drop the batter by large spoonful into the hot oil and press slightly to form a patty shape. Cook until brown on the bottom, and then turn and cook to brown the other side. Continue in batches, adding more oil as needed, until all of the patties are cooked.

Yield varies.

Note: You can use a combination of green and yellow squash for pretty patties. Also, these freeze well, which comes in handy when you have lots of summer squash. Simply freeze the cooked patties and then reheat them in the oven until hot.

Tofu Cutlets

1 package (16 ounces) firm tofu, rinsed and well drained
¼ cup lemon juice or apple cider vinegar
2 T. soy sauce
½ tsp. dry mustard
¼ tsp. pepper

Preheat the oven to 350°.

Cut the block of tofu lengthwise into 8 slices. Arrange the tofu in a single layer in an unoiled glass baking dish. Combine the remaining ingredients in a jar with a tight-fitting lid; shake well. Pour over the tofu.

Bake uncovered for 60 minutes, turning slices halfway through.

Serve them hot or refrigerate them and use the slices in sandwiches, added to salads, or as a tasty snack.

Yield 8 slices.

Tomato Pie

1 unbaked pie shell
3 T. Dijon mustard
1 lb. tomatoes, skinned and sliced
2 eggs
½ cup heavy cream
Salt and pepper to taste
½ cup Gruyère or Swiss cheese, shredded

Preheat the oven to 350°.

Spread the mustard evenly over the bottom of the pie shell. Place the tomatoes over the mustard, overlapping the slices so they all fit.

In a small mixing bowl, combine the eggs, cream, salt, and pepper. Blend well. Pour the egg mixture over the tomatoes and sprinkle with the shredded cheese.

Bake for 30 to 40 minutes or until the custard is set.

Serves 6.

Tuna Patties with Ginger Dressing and Papaya Salsa

For the ginger dressing:
1 cup plain yogurt
2 T. lime juice
1 T. freshly grated ginger
1 T. coarse-grain mustard
2 tsp. oil
½ tsp. cumin

For the papaya salsa:
1½ cups papaya, diced
½ cup chopped red bell peppers
2 T. chopped fresh cilantro
1 T. lime juice
1 T. honey
¼ tsp. ground red pepper

For the tuna patties:
2 cans (6⅛ ounces each) water-packed albacore tuna, drained and flaked
2 eggs, beaten
¼ cup scallions, chopped
1 cup dry bread crumbs, divided
1 T. oil

To make the ginger dressing: In a small bowl, whisk together all of the ingredients and set aside.

To make the papaya salsa: In a small mixing bowl, gently combine all ingredients and set aside.

To make the tuna patties: In a large bowl, combine the tuna, eggs, scallions, ⅔ cup of the bread crumbs, and ¼ cup of the ginger dressing. Shape tuna mixture into 4 patties. Coat with the remaining ⅓ cup of bread crumbs.

Heat the oil, and on medium-low heat, fry patties, turning once, until golden brown, about 4 minutes per side.

To serve, set patties on individual plates, drizzle with the remaining dressing, and top with papaya salsa (or serve it on the side).

Serves 4.

Turkey Burgers

1 lb. ground turkey
2 cloves garlic, minced
3 T. fresh parsley, minced (or 3 tsp. dried parsley)
2 T. fresh rosemary, minced (or 1 tsp. dried rosemary)
Salt and pepper
Butter lettuce leaves
1 tomato, thinly sliced
1 avocado, peeled, pitted, and thinly sliced

Combine the turkey, garlic, parsley, rosemary, salt, and pepper.

Divide the meat mixture into four equal portions; flatten each one into burger patties.

Add about 1 tablespoon of oil to a frying pan and cook the burgers for 5 to 6 minutes. Turn them over and cook the second side for 5 to 6 minutes or until cooked through.

Place each burger on a large lettuce leaf and top with a tomato slice and some avocado slices. Fold over lettuce to hold the burger and toppings in place to eat.

You can also eat these burgers plain or on whole wheat buns or English muffins.

Serves 4.

Vegetable Quesadillas

½ onion, thinly sliced
1 T. oil
1 clove garlic, minced
½ cup mushrooms, thinly sliced
2 carrots, julienned
1 zucchini or other summer squash, thinly sliced
1 bell pepper (any color, or a combination), thinly sliced
Salt and pepper
12 corn tortillas
1½ cups Pepper Jack cheese, shredded

Preheat the oven to 400°.

In a large frying pan, sauté the onion in the oil for 2 minutes. Add the garlic, mushrooms, carrots, zucchini, and bell pepper and cook for 5 minutes more or just until the vegetables are crisp yet tender. Salt and pepper to taste.

To assemble the quesadillas: Place 4 tortillas on a large baking sheet. Place a scoop of vegetables on each tortilla and then add some shredded cheese. Repeat these layers, ending with a third tortilla on top. Press down lightly on top of each tortilla to even out the layers. You'll wind up with 4 quesadillas total.

Bake for 12 to 15 minutes or until the cheese is melted and the quesadillas are hot.

Serve as is, or garnish with salsa, sour cream, or guacamole.

Yields 4 quesadillas.

LUNCHES AND
LIGHT FARE

White Bean and Garlic Spread

1 can (15 ounces) white beans (great northern or cannellini), rinsed and
    drained
2 T. toasted sesame seeds
2 T. chopped onion
2 small cloves garlic, peeled
1 T. lemon juice
2 T. olive or avocado oil
⅛ tsp. hot pepper sauce (i.e. Tabasco sauce)

In a food processor or blender, combine all ingredients and process until smooth. Place the spread in a serving bowl, cover, and refrigerate for several hours until well chilled and flavors have melded.

Serve with fresh vegetables, whole wheat pita bread wedges, crackers, or tortilla chips.

Yields a scant 2 cups.

White Bean and Tomato Dip

1 can (15 ounces) great northern beans, rinsed and drained
¼ cup lemon juice
2 T. dried bread crumbs
2 cloves garlic, peeled
½ tsp. basil
⅛ tsp. ground red pepper or red pepper flakes
6 sun-dried tomato halves, finely diced

Process all ingredient except for the sun-dried tomatoes in a food processor until smooth. Stir in the tomatoes; cover and chill thoroughly before serving with pita bread wedges, crackers, or tortilla chips.

Yield 2 cups.

LUNCHES AND
LIGHT FARE

Zucchini Pizza Bites

3 medium zucchinis
Olive oil for brushing
¼ cup pizza sauce
⅓ cup mozzarella cheese, shredded
⅓ cup mini pepperonis
Oregano for sprinkling

Preheat the oven to 400°.

Slice the zucchinis into one-quarter-inch-thick slices and lay them in a single layer on a large baking sheet that has been very lightly buttered or greased. Brush the tops with olive oil. Bake for 5 minutes.

Remove the zucchini bites from the oven and spoon a thin layer of pizza sauce on each slice. Top them with the cheese and pepperonis and then sprinkle on a bit of oregano.

Return to the oven and bake for about 10 minutes longer or until the cheese is melted and bubbly.

Serves 8 to 12 as an appetizer.

LUNCHES AND LIGHT FARE

MAIN DISHES AND CASSEROLES

Asian-Inspired Chicken with Pasta

¾ cup chicken broth
¼ cup rice vinegar
2 T. soy sauce
1 T. fresh ginger, minced
1 T. garlic, minced
¼ tsp. crushed red pepper
½ lb. cooked chicken, cubed
3 cups cooked buckwheat soba noodles or zoodles
   (zoodles recipe on page 80)
⅓ cup fresh cilantro, minced
2 T. lime juice
¼ cup peanuts

Combine the chicken broth, rice vinegar, soy sauce, ginger, garlic, and crushed red pepper; simmer on medium-low heat for about 5 minutes or until lightly simmering. Remove from heat and add the chicken; stir to combine.

Place the hot cooked noodles or zoodles in a large bowl and gently stir in the chicken mixture, cilantro, lime juice, and peanuts. Serve immediately.

Serves 4 to 6.

MAIN DISHES AND
CASSEROLES

Beef and Green Noodle Casserole

1½ lbs. ground beef
1 tsp. salt
½ tsp. pepper
1 can (15 ounces) tomato sauce
1 package (8 ounces) green noodles, cooked according to package
    directions or 4 cups uncooked zoodles (recipe on page 80)
1 cup sour cream
1 package (8 ounces) cream cheese
6 green onions, chopped and including some of the green tops
½ cup grated cheddar cheese

Preheat the oven to 350°.

Brown the meat and drain off grease. Add the salt, pepper, and tomato sauce; stir to mix.

In a mixing bowl, combine the sour cream, cream cheese, and green onions.

Using a lightly buttered ovenproof casserole dish, layer half of the noodles, then half of the cream mixture, and then half of the meat mixture. Repeat these layers one more time. Cover the top with the cheddar cheese and bake uncovered for 25 to 30 minutes.

Serves 6.

Beef Vegetable Loaf

1½ lbs. ground beef
1 egg
1 cup cooked brown rice
¼ cup onion, chopped
1 small carrot, peeled and grated or finely diced
5 T. fresh parsley, minced (or 2 T. dried parsley), divided
1 tsp. salt
⅛ tsp. pepper
½ cup milk
1 T. prepared mustard (optional)
1 T. ketchup (optional)

Mix the ground beef, egg, cooked rice, onion, diced carrot, 4 tablespoons of the parsley (or 1½ tablespoons if using dried), salt, pepper, and milk until well blended. Pat into a bowl-shaped loaf and place in a lightly greased baking pan or casserole dish.

Combine the mustard and ketchup if using, and brush onto the top of the loaf. Sprinkle with remaining parsley.

Bake at 350° for 1 hour or until done.

Serves 6.

MAIN DISHES AND CASSEROLES

115

Cabbage Casserole ✓

1 large head cabbage, chopped
1 lb. ground beef
½ cup onion, diced
½ cup green bell pepper, chopped (optional)
¼ cup cooked rice (optional)
1 can (46 ounces) tomato juice
1½ cups sour cream
1 cup cheddar cheese, shredded

Bring a large pot of water to a boil; add the cabbage and simmer for 5 to 7 minutes. Drain the cabbage.

In a saucepan, brown the ground beef; drain off excess fat. Add the onion and bell pepper and cook, stirring often, for about 5 minutes or until the onion is slightly softened. Remove from heat and stir in rice if using.

In a large mixing bowl, combine the tomato juice and sour cream, and then add the meat mixture and cabbage; stir to mix. Pour into a large baking dish and cover tightly with aluminum foil.

Bake at 400° for 40 to 45 minutes. Remove the foil and sprinkle on the cheddar cheese and continue to bake, uncovered, for another 15 minutes or until the cheese is melted and bubbly.

Serves 6 to 8.

MAIN DISHES AND CASSEROLES

Chicken and Spinach Enchiladas

1 T. oil
4 boneless skinless chicken breasts, cut into bite-sized pieces
¼ cup onion, diced
1 package (10 ounces) frozen chopped spinach, thawed and squeezed dry
1 can (10¾ ounces) cream of mushroom soup
¾ cup milk
1 cup sour cream
½ tsp. nutmeg
1 tsp. garlic powder
1 tsp. onion powder
8 whole wheat or low-carb tortillas
2 cups mozzarella cheese, shredded
Fresh parsley, minced, for garnish

Preheat the oven to 350°.

In a large saucepan set on medium, heat the oil and add the chicken and onion. Cook, stirring often, for about 7 to 8 minutes or until the chicken is no longer pink. Remove from heat and add the spinach; mix well.

In a mixing bowl, combine the soup, milk, sour cream, nutmeg, garlic powder, and onion powder. Stir ¾ of a cup into the chicken and spinach mixture. Divide this mixture evenly among the 8 tortillas. Roll the tortillas up and place them seam side down in a lightly oiled baking dish. Spoon the remaining soup mixture over the enchiladas.

Cover and bake for 30 minutes. Uncover the baking dish, sprinkle the enchiladas with the cheese, and return to the oven to continue baking for another 15 minutes or until the cheese is melted and bubbly. Remove from the oven and sprinkle with fresh parsley if using.

Yields 8 enchiladas.

MAIN DISHES AND CASSEROLES

Chicken Cacciatore

¼ cup olive oil
6 boneless skinless chicken breasts
1 large onion, diced
2 cloves garlic, minced
2 cans (15 ounces each) tomato sauce
1 can (14½ ounces) diced tomatoes, undrained
1 tsp. salt
¼ tsp. pepper
½ tsp. celery salt or celery seed
½ tsp. basil, rounded
½ tsp. oregano, rounded
2 bay leaves
¼ cup cooking sauterne or dry white wine (optional)

In a large, deep-sided frying pan with a tight-fitting lid, heat oil; add chicken pieces and brown slowly, turning once.

Remove chicken and cook onion and garlic in oil until tender, but not brown. Add the remaining ingredients, except for the cooking wine, and stir to mix.

Return the browned chicken to the pan, cover the pan, and simmer 45 minutes, being careful to not let the sauce bubble hard. Stir in wine if using and simmer uncovered an additional 20 minutes or until the chicken is fork tender. Discard the bay leaves and serve over whole wheat pasta or zoodles (recipe on page 80) with grated Parmesan cheese.

Serves 6 to 8.

Chicken Fajitas

2 T. olive oil
3 boneless skinless chicken breasts, cut into bite-sized pieces (about 1 lb. total)
1 large onion, thinly sliced
1 green bell pepper, seeded, cut in half lengthwise, and thinly sliced
1 orange or yellow bell pepper, seeded, cut in half lengthwise, and thinly sliced
8 ounces mushrooms, sliced
2 large tomatoes, cut in large, bite-sized pieces
¼ cup water, divided
½ tsp. chili powder (more or less depending on the amount of spiciness desired)
½ tsp. garlic powder
½ tsp. cumin
½ tsp. oregano
Salt and pepper to taste
1 T. lemon or lime juice
Whole wheat or low-carb tortillas
Cheddar cheese and sour cream for garnish

In a large skillet, add the olive oil and chicken and cook on medium heat until browned.

Add the onion, bell peppers, mushrooms, and tomatoes. Turn the heat to medium-high and continue to cook, stirring often, for 5 minutes. Add ⅛ cup of water, turn down the heat to medium, cover the skillet, and allow the chicken and vegetables to continue cooking (adding a small amount of water if it starts getting too dry) for 5 to 10 minutes or until the vegetables are somewhat tender and the chicken is cooked completely.

Turn the heat up a bit and add the chili powder, garlic powder, cumin, oregano, salt, pepper, the remaining water, and lemon juice. Continue cooking, uncovered, until the liquid has mostly evaporated, about another 3 minutes. Taste and adjust seasonings as desired. (Some of us like it spicy!)

MAIN DISHES AND CASSEROLES

Serve rolled in tortillas, with cheese and sour cream if desired.

Serves 6 to 8.

Note: This fajita mixture is also good eaten plain without the tortillas, and it reheats beautifully if you have leftovers.

Creamy Baked Chicken and Asparagus

1½ lbs. fresh asparagus spears, woody ends trimmed, and cut in half
4 boneless skinless chicken breasts
2 T. oil
½ tsp. salt
¼ tsp. pepper
1 can (10¾ ounces) cream of chicken soup
½ cup mayonnaise
1 tsp. lemon juice
½ tsp. curry powder
1 cup cheddar cheese, shredded

Partially cook the asparagus by plunging into boiling water and simmering for 2 minutes. Drain and rinse under cold running water until cool enough to handle. Place the asparagus in a greased or buttered 9-inch square baking dish.

In a skillet over medium heat, brown the chicken in the oil, turning to brown the second side. Season the chicken with salt and pepper and arrange the chicken on top of the asparagus.

In a mixing bowl, combine the soup, mayonnaise, lemon juice, and curry powder; pour over the chicken.

Cover and bake in a preheated 375° oven for 40 minutes or until the chicken is cooked completely and is tender. Turn off the oven, remove the chicken, and sprinkle the cheese over the top.

MAIN DISHES AND CASSEROLES

Return to the still-hot oven until the cheese has melted, about 5 minutes more.

Serves 4 to 6.

Garbanzo Burger Patties

½ cup carrots, peeled and finely diced
1 cup zucchini, finely chopped
1 celery stalk, finely chopped
3 T. onion, finely chopped
1 cup garbanzo bean flour (aka chickpea flour)
2 T. oil, plus more oil for frying
2 tsp. Italian herb seasoning
1 whole egg plus 1 egg white
Salt and pepper to taste
8 low-carb (gluten-free) burger buns or English muffins

Place the carrots, zucchini, celery, and onion in a food processor and pulse to finely chop. Add the garbanzo bean flour, 2 tablespoons oil, Italian seasoning, egg, egg white, and a small amount of salt and pepper. Pulse until the ingredients form a smooth, thick batter.

Heat oil in a large skillet over medium heat; drop the batter by large spoonfuls to form 8 patties about half an inch thick. Cook about 4 minutes on each side. Serve in toasted buns or English muffins, dressed as you would a beef burger.

Serves 8.

MAIN DISHES AND CASSEROLES

Halibut Florentine

2 T. butter
2 T. flour
1 cup milk
1 lb. halibut fillets
1 cup water
4 T. lemon juice
1¼ cups finely chopped spinach, cooked and drained
¾ cup sharp cheddar cheese, shredded and divided
3 green onions, chopped
Salt and pepper to taste
1 T. butter, at room temperature

Preheat the oven to 400°.

In a small saucepan, melt 2 tablespoons of butter on medium-low heat. Whisk in the flour and then add the milk, continuing to whisk constantly. Raise the heat to medium and cook, stirring, until the mixture thickens and begins to boil. Remove the white sauce from the heat and add salt and pepper to taste.

Place the halibut fillets in a shallow saucepan. Add the water and lemon juice, cover, and boil for 5 minutes. Remove the fish with a slotted spoon and place in a lightly buttered baking dish.

Continue boiling the cooking broth, uncovered, until it's reduced to two thirds. Add the white sauce, spinach, ¼ cup of the cheese, and the green onions. Bring back up to just a boil, stirring constantly, and then quickly remove from heat. Sprinkle the fillets with salt and pepper. Pour the sauce over the halibut and sprinkle with the remaining cheese. Dot with butter and bake until golden brown, about 8 to 10 minutes.

Serves 4.

Hot Sauce Beef Steak

1½ lbs. round steak, chopped into small, bite-sized pieces
2 T. butter (or 1 T. butter and 1 T. oil)
½ onion, diced
1 tsp. salt
¼ tsp. chili powder
Dash of cayenne pepper
1 clove garlic, minced
¼ tsp. cinnamon
½ cup celery, chopped
2 T. prepared mustard
1½ cups water
2 cups cooked brown rice, divided into 4 servings

Brown steak in the butter. Stir in all of the remaining ingredients. Cover and simmer for 30 minutes or until the meat is tender. If too much water evaporates during cooking, add a small amount so when you ladle it over the rice, there's plenty of broth. (I like to eat it with a spoon!)

Serves 4.

MAIN DISHES AND
CASSEROLES

Italian Sausage and White Bean Cassoulet

1 T. olive oil
½ lb. sweet Italian sausage
1 lb. kielbasa sausage, cut into ½-inch slices
3 leeks, white and pale green parts, sliced
3 cloves garlic, minced
1 apple, peeled, cored, and chopped
1 T. fresh rosemary (or ½ tsp. dried)
1 tsp. sage
1 bay leaf
1 can (14½ ounces) diced tomatoes, undrained
2 to 3 drops hot pepper sauce (such as Tabasco)
2 cans (15 ounces each) great northern beans, rinsed and drained
1 package (10 ounces) frozen baby lima beans, rinsed and drained
1½ cups chicken broth
2 T. tomato paste
Pepper to taste
½ cup chopped fresh parsley

Preheat the oven to 350°.

In a Dutch oven or heavy-bottom pot over medium heat, warm the oil and then add the Italian sausage. Brown for about 10 minutes, turning occasionally. Add the kielbasa sausage and brown both types of sausage about 10 minutes longer. Transfer to a plate and slice the Italian sausages ½-inch thick.

Add the leeks and garlic to the same pot and sauté until soft, about 5 minutes. Add the apple, rosemary, sage, and bay leaf. Stir in the diced tomatoes, hot pepper sauce, white beans, lima beans, broth, tomato paste, and sausages. Season with pepper.

Bake, covered, about 1 hour. Remove lid and stir in parsley. Bake, uncovered, for 15 minutes longer. Remove bay leaf before serving.

Serves 6 to 8.

Leftover Turkey and Wild Rice Casserole

6 cups cooked wild rice (recipe on page 80)
3 cups cooked turkey, cut into bite-sized pieces
1 can (10¾ ounces) cream of mushroom soup
3 celery stalks, sliced
1 cup mushrooms, sliced
1 onion, chopped
1 cup sour cream
½ cup (1 stick) butter, melted
1 tsp. salt
¼ tsp. pepper

Preheat the oven to 350°.

In a large mixing bowl, combine all of the ingredients. Spoon into a greased or buttered large rectangular baking dish.

Cover and bake for 45 minutes. Uncover and continue baking for another 15 minutes or until the top is golden brown.

Serves 6 to 8.

Mexican Meat Loaf

2 lbs. ground beef
2 carrots, peeled and grated
1 green onion, minced
1 tsp. salt
1 egg, beaten
2 T. jalapeno peppers, minced
½ cup salsa

Add all ingredients in a large mixing bowl and mix well.

Pack into a loaf pan and bake at 375° for 1 hour.

Serves 6 to 8.

MAIN DISHES AND
CASSEROLES

125

Pork Chops and White Bean Casserole

2 cups (1 lb.) dried white beans
2 tsp. salt
¼ tsp. pepper
2 bay leaves
2 to 3 cloves garlic, minced
1 T. butter
2 cups onion, diced
2 cans (14½ ounces each) diced tomatoes, or 5 large tomatoes, chopped
1 tsp. oregano
1 tsp. thyme
6 pork chops

Early in the morning: Cover the beans with cold water in a container, put on its lid, and refrigerate all day until about 3 hours before dinnertime.

Drain off the water, and then put the beans in a large pot. Add 5 cups fresh water, salt, pepper, bay leaves, and garlic. Bring to a boil and then reduce the heat. Cover and simmer for 1 hour, stirring occasionally. Drain and remove the bay leaves.

Meanwhile, sauté in butter the onion, tomatoes, oregano, and thyme and cook for several minutes. Stir this mixture together with the beans and turn into a large ovenproof casserole dish.

Brown the pork chops in a skillet and then tuck them into the bean mixture, making sure the chops are covered.

Bake, covered, at 350° for 1½ hours and then uncover and continue baking for another 15 minutes.

Serves 6.

Rice and Lentil Casserole

1 cup brown rice
¾ cup lentils
4 cups water
¼ cup onion, diced
3 tsp. beef bouillon
¼ tsp. oregano
½ tsp. basil
¼ tsp. garlic powder
½ cup cheddar cheese, shredded

In a mixing bowl, stir together all of the ingredients except for the cheese.

Pour the mixture into a 2-quart casserole or soufflé dish and bake, covered, at 375° for 2 hours. Uncover and sprinkle on the cheese; bake uncovered for another 15 to 20 minutes or until the cheese is melted and bubbly and the rice and lentils are cooked through.

Serves 6.

Savory Roasted Leg of Lamb

1½ tsp. soy sauce
1 T. oil
2½ tsp. fresh thyme, minced (or ¾ tsp. dried)
1½ tsp. fresh marjoram, minced (or ½ tsp. dried)
1 tsp. rosemary, fresh or dried
1 tsp. salt
½ tsp. pepper
½ tsp. ground ginger
1 bay leaf, broken, but in large enough pieces to pick out after roasting
1 leg of lamb, 5 to 7 lbs.
2 cloves garlic, sliced into quarters or thirds, depending on size and taste

Preheat the oven to 350°.

In a small bowl, combine all of the ingredients except for the leg of lamb and the garlic.

Cut small slits in the lamb and insert the garlic slivers. Then rub the spices mixture over the surface of the lamb.

Roast the lamb, uncovered, for 20 to 25 minutes per pound. Remove from the oven and allow the lamb to sit for 10 minutes before carving.

Serves 8.

Sole in Oyster and Shrimp Sauce

6 fillets of sole (about 2½ lbs.)
3 T. lemon juice
1 tsp. salt
⅛ tsp. pepper
2 T. butter
½ cup dry white wine
1 small onion, sliced
1 bay leaf
½ tsp. dried tarragon leaves

For sauce:
10 ounces oysters
3 T. butter
½ lb. fresh mushroom, sliced
3 T. flour
1 cup reserved fish stock
½ cup dry white wine
2 egg yolks, slightly beaten
½ cup heavy cream
½ cup cooked salad shrimp

Preheat the oven to 350°.

To prepare the fish: Rinse the fillets under cold water. Dry well on paper towels. Fold the fillets over in thirds and arrange them in a single layer in a lightly buttered baking dish. Sprinkle with lemon juice, salt, and pepper. Dot with butter. Pour wine over all, top with onion, bay leaf, and tarragon.

Bake, uncovered, for 20 minutes or until the fish flakes easily when tested with fork. With a slotted spatula, lift the fillets to a large, shallow serving dish and keep warm, reserving 1 cup cooking stock.

To prepare the sauce: While the fish is baking, in a small saucepan, cook the oysters in their liquid just until edges begin to curl. Drain and set aside.

Melt the butter in a medium saucepan. Add the mushrooms and sauté, stirring occasionally, about 5 minutes. Remove from heat and stir in the flour until smooth. Add the reserved fish stock and wine and then cook over medium heat, stirring constantly, until mixture comes to a boil. Reduce the heat and simmer for 3 minutes.

In a medium bowl, combine the egg yolks and cream; mix well. Stir in a little of the hot mushroom mixture. Slowly pour back into the saucepan and cook, stirring, for several minutes or until slightly thickened Add the cooked oysters and shrimp. Pour the sauce over the fillets and serve immediately.

Serves 6.

MAIN DISHES AND CASSEROLES

Soybean Casserole

1 cup dried soybeans (soaked overnight in water to cover by 2 inches)
2 T. diced salt pork or bacon
1 cup celery, sliced
2 T. green onions, chopped
1 T. green bell or other sweet pepper
3 T. flour
1 cup milk
½ tsp. salt
¼ cup wheat germ

Rinse the soaked soybeans and place in a large pot and drain; cover with fresh water and bring to a boil. Simmer soybeans for 1½ to 2 hours, adding boiling water if needed to keep them covered. Drain and set aside.

Preheat the oven to 350°.

Brown the salt pork or bacon in a frying pan. Add celery, green onions, and green pepper and cook for 5 minutes. Stir in the flour and then slowly add the milk, stirring constantly. Add the salt, and, while continuing to stir constantly, bring the mixture to a low boil.

Stir in the cooked soybeans and pour the mixture into a lightly buttered casserole dish. Sprinkle the wheat germ over the top and bake for 30 to 40 minutes.

Serves 4 to 6.

MAIN DISHES AND
CASSEROLES

Spinach Casserole

¾ cup cooked brown rice, cooled
½ cup cheddar cheese, shredded
2 eggs, beaten
2 T. parsley, minced (or use 2 tsp. dried parsley)
½ tsp. salt
¼ tsp. pepper
1 lb. fresh spinach, chopped
2 T. wheat germ
1 T. butter, melted

Preheat the oven to 350°.

In a medium bowl, combine the rice and cheese.

In a large bowl, combine the eggs, parsley, salt, and pepper. Stir to mix. Add the rice and cheese mixture and stir again. Next, add the spinach and stir to mix well. Pour the mixture into an oiled or buttered casserole dish.

In a small cup (a teacup works well), mix the wheat germ and melted butter and then sprinkle this mixture over the spinach mixture.

Bake for 35 minutes.

Serves 4 to 6.

MAIN DISHES AND
CASSEROLES

Stuffed Acorn Squash

3 acorn squashes, halved and seeded
½ cup water
¾ lb. ground beef
3 T. onion, finely diced
3 T. celery, finely chopped
2 T. flour
½ tsp. salt
½ tsp. sage
¾ cup milk
1 cup cooked brown rice, millet, or barley
¾ cup cheddar cheese, shredded

Invert the squash in a large baking dish. Add water and cover with foil. Bake at 375° for 50 to 60 minutes or until tender. When the squash is done, remove from the oven and then turn down the heat to 350°.

While the squash is baking, brown the ground beef with the onion and celery until no longer pink. Drain most of the fat. Stir in the flour, salt, and sage until blended and then add the milk, stirring constantly. Bring to a boil, reduce the heat, and simmer, still stirring constantly, for about 2 minutes or until thickened and bubbly. Stir in the rice.

Transfer the squash, cut side up, to a lightly oiled baking sheet. Fill the cavities with the meat mixture. Bake at 350° for 30 minutes. Remove from the oven, sprinkle with the cheese, and bake about 5 minutes longer or until the cheese is completely melted.

Serves 6.

MAIN DISHES AND
CASSEROLES

Tilapia Piccata

Note: You can substitute sole fillets for the tilapia.

2 lbs. tilapia fillets, rinsed and patted dry
Salt and pepper
2 T. flour, more or less, for dredging fish
2 T. butter
4 T. lemon juice
3 T. fresh parsley, minced
1 T. capers, drained
1 lemon, sliced thin for garnish

Season the tilapia lightly with salt and pepper. Dredge the fillets in the flour.

Heat the butter in a skillet. Add the tilapia and cook the fish until golden brown, about 5 minutes. Turn and cook the second side until the fish flakes with a fork. Drain the fillets on paper towels, plate them, and keep them warm.

In the same skillet, add the lemon juice, parsley, and capers and heat thoroughly, about 30 seconds. Pour the pan juices over the fish and top each with lemon slices for garnish.

Serves 4 to 6.

MAIN DISHES AND CASSEROLES

Tofu Enchiladas

For the filling:
1 small onion, diced
3 cloves garlic
1 tsp. butter or oil
½ tsp. salt
1 tsp. (scant) cumin
¼ cup soy sauce
1 block firm tofu

For the sauce:
1 small can green chili salsa
1 can (15 ounces) tomato sauce

For the tortillas:
8 corn tortillas, more or less
Oil for frying tortillas (about ⅛ cup total)
Cheddar cheese, shredded

Preheat the oven to 350°.

To make the filling: In a large frying pan, sauté the onion and garlic in butter or oil. Season with the salt, cumin, and soy sauce. Add a diced or slightly mashed brick of tofu. Heat through a few minutes but don't overcook.

To make the sauce: In a medium saucepan, mix together and heat the green chili salsa and tomato sauce.

Preparing the enchiladas: Fry the tortillas in oil, but don't make them hard—they must be limp in order to roll. Fill each tortilla with some of the tofu mixture and place seam-side down in a baking dish. Pour the salsa mixture over the enchiladas and top with the cheese.

Bake just until the cheese is melted and bubbly and the enchiladas are heated thoroughly.

Serves 6.

MAIN DISHES AND CASSEROLES

White Chicken Chili

1 lb. boneless skinless chicken breasts, cut into bite-sized pieces
1 onion, diced
2 cloves garlic, minced
1 T. oil
2 cans (15½ ounces each) white beans, rinsed and drained
1 can (14½ ounces) chicken broth
2 cans (4 ounces each) diced green chilies
1 tsp. salt
1 tsp. cumin
1 tsp. oregano
½ tsp. pepper
¼ tsp. cayenne pepper
1 cup sour cream
½ cup heavy whipping cream

In a large saucepan, cook the chicken, onion, and garlic in the oil until chicken is no longer pink.

Add the beans, broth, diced chilies, and seasonings. Bring to a boil; reduce the heat and simmer, uncovered, for about 30 minutes. Remove from the heat and stir in the sour cream and whipping cream. Serve immediately.

You can garnish the chili with jack cheese, avocados, fresh diced tomatoes, or crumbled tortilla chips.

Serves 6 to 8.

MAIN DISHES AND CASSEROLES

SALADS AND SALAD DRESSINGS

Apple Salad with Buttermilk Dressing

²/₃ cup buttermilk
½ cup plain yogurt
2 T. apple cider vinegar
1 tsp. tarragon (or 1 T. fresh tarragon leaves)
¼ tsp. salt
¼ tsp. pepper
4 apples, cored and sliced (If you use a combination of apples, the varying colors of the peels will add visual appeal.)
1 large head lettuce, torn

To make the salad dressing: In a medium bowl, whisk together the buttermilk, yogurt, vinegar, tarragon, salt, and pepper.

In another bowl, place the apple slices and ¼ cup of the salad dressing and gently toss to coat the apples.

To serve, gently toss the apples with the torn lettuce leaves and bring to the table along with the remaining salad dressing on the side.

Serves 6.

Asian-Inspired Salad Dressing

2 T. soy sauce
2 T. vinegar (regular white or rice vinegar)
2 T. water
½ cup oil
½ tsp. dry mustard
1 tsp. ginger

Combine all ingredients and vigorously whisk or shake to mix well. Use immediately or refrigerate until needed.

Yields about ¾ cup.

SALADS AND SALAD DRESSINGS

Avocado and Mushroom Piquant

½ lb. small button mushrooms
2 avocados
½ cup oil
3 T. tarragon vinegar
2 T. lemon juice
2 T. water
1 T. minced fresh parsley
1 clove garlic, minced
¾ tsp. salt
Pepper to taste
Whole lettuce leaves

Remove the stems from the mushrooms. Peel and slice or cube the avocados. Place both in a salad bowl.

Combine remaining ingredients except for the lettuce leaves and pour over avocados and mushrooms. Cover bowl tightly and chill for several hours, spooning the dressing over the vegetables several times. Serve on lettuce leaves.

Serves 4 to 6.

SALADS AND
SALAD DRESSINGS

Caesar Salad Dressing

4 anchovy fillets
$2/3$ cup mayonnaise
4 cloves garlic, minced
Kosher or coarse salt
2 T. lemon juice
1 tsp. Dijon mustard
1 tsp. Worcestershire sauce
1 ounce finely grated Parmesan cheese
Freshly ground black pepper to taste
1 T. water

Stack the anchovies and cut lengthwise into very thin strips; next, cut them into tiny dices. Last, take a fork and mash the anchovy dices until a paste is made.

Place all of the ingredients, including the anchovy paste, into a bowl and whisk until well blended. Covered tightly, the Caesar salad dressing will stay fresh in the refrigerator for up to two weeks.

Yields ¾ cup.

Caribbean Salad with Pork and Melon

For the dressing:
1 tsp. Caribbean jerk seasoning
2 T. white wine vinegar
1 T. olive oil

For the salad:
1 lb. boneless pork chops
1 T. Caribbean jerk seasoning
1 T. butter
1 T. oil
6 cups salad greens
½ bell pepper, cut into thin strips
½ small cantaloupe, peeled and seeded, cubed

To make the dressing: Place all dressing ingredients in a jar that has a tight-fitting lid and shake well. Refrigerate until serving time.

To prepare the pork: Rub the pork chops on both sides with jerk seasoning. In a skillet, melt the butter and oil until hot; add the pork. Cook over medium heat, turning occasionally, until browned and cooked through, about 15 minutes. Remove from heat and slice the pork in thin strips.

To assemble the salad: Toss the salad greens, pork, bell pepper, and cantaloupe together with the dressing and serve immediately.

Serves 4 to 6.

SALADS AND
SALAD DRESSINGS

Celeriac and Spinach Salad

1 T. apple cider vinegar

¼ cup light oil (avocado or sunflower oil is good in this recipe, but you can use olive oil)

Salt and pepper to taste

1 medium celeriac (also called celery root), washed well, skinned, and thinly sliced into sticks

3 celery ribs, sliced diagonally

½ cup baby spinach leaves

3 radishes, sliced

In a large bowl, whisk together the vinegar, oil, salt, and pepper. Add the remaining ingredients and gently toss to coat.

Serves 4.

Chicken Couscous Salad

1½ cups chicken broth

3 tsp. soy sauce, divided

1 tsp. oil (use sesame oil if you have it, olive oil if you don't)

1 cup uncooked wheat couscous

1 cup fresh peas, shelled (or 1½ cups sugar snap or snow peas)

¾ cup broccoli florets, chopped if necessary to make bite-sized pieces

2 green onions, sliced

1 red bell pepper, chopped

1 cup cooked chicken, cut into bite-sized pieces

¼ cup lemon juice

2 T. olive oil (or use 1 T. each, olive and sesame oil)

¼ tsp. pepper

¼ cup slivered almonds

1 T. sesame seeds

In a large saucepan, combine the chicken broth, 1 teaspoon soy sauce, and oil; bring to a gentle boil.

Remove the pot from the heat and add the couscous. Cover the pot with a lid, and let it stand for 20 minutes. Fluff with a fork and then place the couscous in a large bowl.

In a double boiler, steam the peas, broccoli, green onions, and bell pepper for about 2 minutes. Rinse under cold tap water to cool the vegetables, drain well, and then add to the couscous. Add the chicken.

Combine the lemon juice, oil, 2 teaspoons soy sauce, and pepper and whisk or shake contents in a covered jar to mix thoroughly. Pour onto the couscous and mix well.

Right before serving, add the almonds and sesame seeds.

Serves 4 to 6.

Chicken Salad with Curried Yogurt Dressing

For the dressing:
1 cup plain yogurt
¾ tsp. curry powder
2 T. honey
½ tsp. lemon and herb seasoning

For the salad:
4 to 6 cups mixed greens
2 cups cooked chicken, chopped
1 medium avocado, sliced
2 to 4 T. almond slices
1 can mandarin oranges, drained

Combine ingredients for dressing and mix well.

In a large mixing bowl or salad bowl, layer the salad ingredients. Spoon dressing over the salad and gently toss to mix. (There is usually dressing left over, so use most of the dressing, toss, and then taste to see if you have enough.)

Serves 4 to 6.

Citrusy Crab (or Shrimp) Salad

For the dressing:

¼ tsp. grated orange peel

2 T. orange juice

1 T. balsamic vinegar

2 tsp. olive oil

½ tsp. fresh tarragon (or ⅛ tsp. dried)

For the salad:

2½ cups torn greens (a combination of lettuce and spinach works well)

½ cup cabbage, shredded or thinly sliced

1 orange, peeled and sectioned

¼ cup sweet onion, thinly sliced and separated into rings

6 ounces cooked crabmeat, cut into bite-sized pieces, or cooked salad shrimp

To make the dressing: In a small bowl, whisk together all dressing ingredients; set aside.

To assemble the salad: Combine the salad greens, cabbage, orange sections, and onion. Toss gently to mix. Add the crabmeat and gently toss again. Pour the dressing over the salad mixture and gently toss to coat.

Serves 4.

Creamy Avocado Salad Dressing

1 avocado, peeled
1 cup plain yogurt
¼ cup red onion, finely diced
3 T. lemon juice
2 T. olive oil
1 clove garlic, minced
1 tsp. dill weed or 1 T. fresh dill
½ tsp. salt
Pinch of cayenne pepper

Place all of the ingredients in a blender or food processor and blend until creamy and smooth. Taste and adjust seasonings as needed.

Will keep in the refrigerator for 3 to 4 days.

Yields about 1½ cups.

Creamy Vinaigrette

3 T. olive oil
1 T. white wine vinegar
1 tsp. Dijon mustard
¼ tsp. salt
⅛ tsp. pepper
2 T. heavy cream

Whisk together all of the ingredients until well blended.

Yields 1 to 2 servings.

Despacio Salad

1 lb. ground beef
1 can (15 ounces) kidney beans, rinsed and drained
1 onion, diced
4 large tomatoes, skinned and chopped
1 avocado, peeled and cubed
1 can (2¼ ounces) sliced black olives, drained
1 head lettuce, torn (about 6 or 7 cups)
½ cup cheddar cheese, shredded (can use more if desired)
1 cup tortilla chips (regular or nacho cheese flavored)
French dressing, or dressing of your choice

In a medium saucepan, cook the ground beef thoroughly. Drain off the fat and cool.

In a large bowl, gently toss together the meat, kidney beans, onion, tomatoes, avocado, olives, and lettuce.

Right before serving, add the cheese and tortilla chips and dress with French dressing.

Serves 6 to 8.

Notes:

Dijon Vinaigrette with Tarragon

½ cup olive oil
⅓ cup red wine vinegar
2 tsp. dried tarragon
1 tsp. Dijon mustard
1 clove garlic, minced
½ tsp. salt
½ tsp. pepper
½ tsp. chives, finely minced
½ tsp. fresh parsley, finely minced

Whisk together all of the ingredients until well blended, or blend in a food processor or blender until smooth.

Yields slightly less than 1 cup.

Green Salad with Fruity Dressing

1 cup fresh strawberries, divided
¼ cup ranch dressing
1 T. mayonnaise
½ clove (or 1 small clove) garlic, minced
6 cups torn salad greens (use a variety of greens including spinach, lettuce, kale, etc.)
⅓ cup fresh blueberries
⅓ cup seedless red grapes, halved
2 green onions, sliced
½ small red onion, thinly sliced and separated into rings

To make the dressing: In a blender or food processor, puree ½ cup of the strawberries with the ranch dressing, mayonnaise, and garlic. Chill until needed.

To assemble the salad: Combine the salad greens, remaining strawberries, blueberries, grapes, and green onions. Pour or

SALADS AND SALAD DRESSINGS

spoon the dressing over the salad and gently mix to coat. Top with onion rings and serve.

Serves 6.

Herbed Barley and Tomato Salad

1 cup pearled barley
3 cups chicken broth
¼ cup onion, chopped
1 clove garlic, minced
2 T. lemon juice
1 tsp. salt
¼ tsp. pepper
6 large tomatoes
½ cup plain yogurt or sour cream
2 T. fresh parsley, minced
1 T. fresh chives, snipped
1 T. fresh dill weed (or 1 tsp. dried)
Salt and pepper to taste

In a saucepan, combine the barley, chicken broth, onion, garlic, lemon juice, salt, and pepper. Bring to a boil and then reduce the heat. Cover and simmer on low heat for 1 hour or until barley is tender. Cool to room temperature. (I usually refrigerate the cooked barley so it cools faster.)

Cut the tops off the tomatoes and scoop out the pulp; save the tomato shells. Place the tomato pulp into a blender or food processor and process until smooth. You need ½ cup of blended pulp. (Save remainder of the pulp for others uses, such as adding to soups, casseroles, or smoothies.)

Combine the ½ cup of pulp with the yogurt, parsley, chives, and dill weed and stir vigorously by hand to mix well. Add salt and pepper to taste. Pour the dressing over the cooled, cooked

SALADS AND
SALAD DRESSINGS

barley and toss to coat lightly. Fill the tomato shells with the barley salad and serve.

Serves 12 as a side dish or 6 as the main dish.

Marinated Bean Salad

½ onion, minced
1 cup celery, minced
1 tsp. salt
½ cup vinegar
¼ cup oil
1 can green beans (cut, not frenched), drained
1 can garbanzo beans, rinsed and drained
1 can kidney beans, rinsed and drained

Combine the onion, celery, salt, vinegar, and oil. Add the beans and mix to coat the beans completely. Refrigerate for several hours or overnight.

Serve using a large slotted spoon.

Serves 6 to 8.

Oriental Pea and Shrimp Salad

¾ cup mayonnaise
¼ tsp. curry powder
1 T. lemon juice
Garlic salt to taste
2 packages (1 lb. each) frozen peas, thawed and drained
1 cup cooked salad shrimp
1 cup celery, diced
½ cup cashews

Whisk together the mayonnaise, curry powder, lemon juice, and garlic salt.

In a large bowl, gently toss the peas, shrimp, celery, and cashews until combined. Pour the dressing over the pea mixture and gently mix. Serve immediately.

Serves 6 to 8.

Note: If made ahead of time, keep refrigerated and do not add the cashews until right before serving.

Pea, Tomato, and Brown Rice Salad

2 cups hot, cooked brown rice
¾ cup olive oil
3 T. vinegar
Salt and pepper to taste
1 cup green peas, cooked and cooled
2 tomatoes, peeled and chopped
¼ cup fresh parsley, minced
1 T. fresh basil, minced (or 1 tsp. dried basil)

While rice is still hot from cooking, add the olive oil, vinegar, salt and pepper; toss to mix well. Spoon into a serving bowl and allow to cool.

In another bowl, combine the peas, tomatoes, parsley, and basil. Add this mixture to the rice, stir to mix well, and chill salad completely before serving.

Serves 6 to 8.

SALADS AND
SALAD DRESSINGS

Pear and Spinach Salad

¼ cup olive oil
2 T. lemon juice
1 tsp. honey
½ tsp. thyme
Salt and pepper to taste
3 cups spinach
2 Bosc pears, peeled, pared, and sliced
½ cup salted and toasted pumpkin or sunflower seeds
½ cup crumbled Feta or blue cheese

To make the dressing: In a small bowl, whisk together the olive oil, lemon juice, honey, thyme, salt, and pepper.

In a large bowl, gently toss the spinach, pears, and pumpkin seeds. Add the salad dressing and toss gently again. Top with the cheese crumbles and serve immediately.

Serves 4.

Quinoa Salad

1 cup uncooked quinoa
2 cups water or vegetable broth
¼ tsp. salt
1 large tomato, chopped
¼ cup onion, chopped
1 cucumber, peeled, seeded, and chopped
¼ cup pitted black olives, halved
1 avocado, peeled and chopped
¼ cup Italian dressing (or to taste)

Vigorously rinse the quinoa; drain. Place the quinoa in a pot and add the water or broth and salt. Bring it to a boil and then reduce the heat. Cover the pot and simmer for 15 to 20 minutes or until the liquid is absorbed.

Fluff the quinoa and then place it in a large salad or mixing bowl and refrigerate until cool. Add the remaining ingredients and toss gently to mix. Serve immediately or refrigerate until ready to eat.

Serves 6 to 8.

Note: It's necessary to rinse uncooked quinoa well to remove the bitter covering. One cup uncooked quinoa makes about 3 cups cooked.

Quinoa Salad Variation

1 cup uncooked quinoa
2 cups water
¼ tsp. salt
½ cup sunflower seeds
½ cup carrots, chopped or thinly sliced
½ cup fresh parsley
⅛ cup black or green olives, cut in half or quartered
1 tomato, chopped
2 cloves garlic, minced
2 T. olive or avocado oil
2 T. soy sauce
2 T. lemon juice
Salt and pepper to taste

Vigorously rinse the quinoa; drain. Place the quinoa in a pot and add the water and salt. Bring it to a boil and then reduce the heat. Cover the pot and simmer for 15 to 20 minutes or until the liquid is absorbed. Allow the quinoa to cool before tossing with the other ingredients.

In a mixing bowl, combine the cooked quinoa, sunflower seeds, carrots, parsley, olives, tomato, and garlic.

In another bowl, whisk together the oil, soy sauce, and lemon juice (or use a jar with a tight-fitting lid and shake). Pour the dressing over the salad, toss gently, and add salt and pepper to taste.

SALADS AND
SALAD DRESSINGS

You can serve the salad immediately or chill in the refrigerator to help the flavors meld.

Serves 6 to 8.

Note: *It's necessary to rinse uncooked quinoa well to remove the bitter covering. One cup uncooked quinoa makes about 3 cups cooked.*

Spinach Salad

For the dressing:
¼ cup vinegar
2 tsp. soy sauce
½ tsp. dry mustard
½ tsp. curry powder
½ tsp. salt
¼ tsp. pepper
1 clove garlic, minced
1 cup oil

For the salad:
4 to 6 slices bacon
3 eggs, hard-boiled
¼ lb. mushrooms
6 to 8 cups fresh spinach

Place all dressing ingredients into a jar that has a tight-fitting lid and shake vigorously. Refrigerate until needed.

Fry the bacon until crisp, drain on paper towels, and then crumble into bite-sized pieces. Peel and slice or chop the hard-boiled eggs. Slice the mushrooms.

Combine all of the salad ingredients and gently toss to mix. Right before serving, toss the salad with the chilled dressing. (Go a bit light on the dressing because it's strong. Taste and add more if needed.)

Serves 6.

Tabbouleh

1 cup uncooked bulgur or quinoa
¼ cup onion, chopped
2 tomatoes, chopped
½ cup fresh mint or parsley (or a combination), chopped
1 cup fresh vegetables of your choice, diced (cucumbers, bell peppers, carrots, peas, etc.)
2 T. lemon or lime juice
2 T. olive or avocado oil
Salt and pepper to taste

To prepare the grain: For bulgar, rinse and drain. Bring 2 cups water to a boil, add the bulgur, and simmer for about 15 minutes or until the water is absorbed.

For quinoa, vigorously rinse the grains and then bring 2 cups water to a boil. Remove from the heat and stir in the quinoa. Cover the pot and let the mixture stand for 20 minutes. When the grain is cooked, uncover the pot, fluff the quinoa with a fork, and place it in a large bowl.

Chill the grains. When cool, add the vegetables and mix.

Stir together the lemon juice and oil and pour over the salad; toss gently. Add salt and pepper to taste. You can serve this salad chilled or at room temperature.

Serves 6.

SALADS AND
SALAD DRESSINGS

Tomato Mushroom Salad

3 medium tomatoes, cut into wedges
6 medium fresh mushrooms, sliced thin
2 T. fresh parsley, minced
2 T. lemon juice
¼ cup vegetable, olive, or avocado oil
¼ tsp. salt
⅛ tsp. pepper
6 butter lettuce leaves, whole

In a large bowl, combine the tomatoes, mushrooms, and parsley.

In a small jar with a tight-fitting lid, combine the other ingredients except the lettuce and shake vigorously. Pour dressing over tomatoes and mushrooms and gently mix. Chill until serving time.

To serve, place the tomato and mushroom mixture on lettuce leaves.

Serves 6.

Tossed Italian Salad

5 cups torn greens
½ lb. fresh mushrooms, sliced
4 ounces mozzarella cheese, cut in ½-inch cubes
1 cup garbanzo beans, rinsed and drained
½ cup pepperoni, thinly sliced
½ cup Italian salad dressing

Gently toss all of the salad ingredients until mixed and then pour the dressing over everything, toss again, and serve immediately.

Serves 6.

SALADS AND
SALAD DRESSINGS

Vegetable Salad Bowl

For the dressing:
½ cup white vinegar
1 cup olive oil
1½ tsp. salt
¼ tsp. pepper
½ tsp. dry mustard
1 clove garlic, minced
¼ cup fresh parsley, minced

For the salad:
2 cups carrots, thinly sliced
2 cups celery, sliced diagonally
2 cups cucumber, peeled, quartered lengthwise, seeded, and sliced
2 cups thinly sliced cauliflower
1 sweet onion, thinly sliced
1 pint cherry tomatoes, stems removed
¼ cup fresh parsley, minced

In a jar with a tight-fitting lid, combine all of the dressing ingredients. Shake vigorously and refrigerate until well chilled.

Place all of the salad ingredients except the parsley in a large bowl and refrigerate until well chilled.

To serve, mix the vegetables with the dressing and sprinkle the parsley on top.

Yields ½ gallon.

SALADS AND
SALAD DRESSINGS

SOUPS AND STEWS

Barley and Vegetable Soup

¾ cup pearled barley
11 cups chicken broth, divided
3 T. butter
1½ cups onion, minced
1 cup carrots, peeled and thinly sliced
1 cup mushrooms, sliced
½ cup celery, chopped
Salt and pepper to taste

In a saucepan, combine the pearled barley and 3 cups of the chicken broth. Bring to a boil over moderate heat, stirring occasionally, and then turn down the heat. Cover the pot and simmer for about an hour or until the liquid is absorbed and the barley is cooked.

In a large pot, melt the butter over medium-low heat, being careful not to brown the butter. Add the onion, carrots, mushrooms, and celery; sauté until the vegetables are softened.

Add the remainder of the broth (8 cups) and simmer the mixture for 30 minutes. Add the barley and simmer for 5 or 10 minutes more. Add salt and pepper to taste.

Serves 6 to 8.

SOUPS AND
STEWS

Beef and Turnip Stew

¾ lb. beef (bottom round, eye of round, or chuck steak), cubed
2 tsp. olive oil
1 tsp. rosemary
2 medium onions, sliced
3 cloves garlic, minced
2½ cups beef broth
1 T. tomato paste
¼ tsp. pepper
6 turnips, cleaned and cut into ½-inch cubes
4 carrots, peeled and sliced

Brown the beef cubes in the olive oil. When the meat has been browned on all sides, add the rosemary, onions, and garlic and cook for 2 to 3 minutes, stirring constantly. Stir in the broth, tomato paste, and pepper. Cover and cook for about 45 minutes or until the meat is thoroughly cooked and tender.

Add the turnips and carrots and cook about 20 minutes more or until the vegetables are tender, stirring occasionally.

Serves 4 to 6.

SOUPS AND
STEWS

Black Beans with Pork and Citrus Sauce

For the stew:
2 T. olive oil
1 lb. pork, cubed
2 cloves garlic, minced
1 small onion, chopped
1 large or 2 medium tomatoes, skinned and chopped
Salt and pepper to taste
3 cans (15 ounces each) black beans, rinsed and drained
   (use pintos if you prefer)
Beef broth or water as needed (at least a quart or two)
Hot cooked rice for serving

For the citrus sauce:
⅓ cup lemon juice
⅓ cup orange juice
½ tsp. cumin
1 tsp. basil
1 tsp. oregano
2 cloves garlic, minced

To make the stew: In a large, heavy pot, heat the oil and add the pork. Brown all sides and then add the garlic, onion, and tomatoes. Cook, stirring regularly, until the onion and garlic are aromatic. Add the rinsed beans, and enough broth or water to barely cover. Cover the pot with a lid and cook on low heat for several hours so the stew has a chance to thicken a bit. (Although you can eat it much sooner than that—say, after an hour of cooking time.)

To make citrus sauce: Combine all the ingredients in a jar with a tight-fitting lid. Shake hard. Sometimes the spices want to float on top, and the minced garlic likes to drop to the bottom, so I usually take a spoon and mix and scoop when I'm ready to use it.

SOUPS AND STEWS

Notes:

To serve, place hot, cooked rice in the bottom of individual bowls. Add the stew, and then spoon some citrus sauce on top. Don't be shy with the sauce, because it's delicious!

Serves 4 to 6 or more, depending on how much broth and rice you use.

Chicken Goulash

1 whole chicken, cut into pieces
2 cups tomatoes, chopped
2 tsp. salt
3 onions, chopped
1 green bell pepper, seeded and chopped
2 carrots, peeled and sliced or chopped
1 potato, peeled and diced
1-2 T. paprika
Sour cream for serving

Boil the chicken in water to cover until tender, about 2½ hours.

Remove the chicken from the broth so both can cool faster. When cool enough to handle, remove the meat from the skin and bones and cut the meat into bite-sized pieces. Strain off as much of the fat from the broth as you can.

Return the meat to the strained broth, add remaining ingredients (except for the sour cream), and simmer for 1 hour. Taste and adjust seasonings as desired.

To serve, ladle into individual bowls and top each with a dollop of sour cream.

Serves 6.

SOUPS AND STEWS

Chicken, Lentil, and Barley Stew

4 cups chicken broth
½ cup lentils
½ cup pearled barley
1 cup cooked chicken, cubed
½ cup carrots, peeled and diced
½ cup celery, diced
¼ cup onion, diced
Salt, pepper, and parsley to taste

Pour the broth into a pot and add the lentils and barley; simmer, covered, for 1 hour.

Add the remaining ingredients and simmer for at least another 30 minutes or until the barley, lentils, and vegetables are tender. Add more broth or water if the stew begins looking too dry.

Serves 4 to 6.

SOUPS AND STEWS

Chili Verde

2 T. oil
¾ lb. beef chuck or round roast, cubed
¾ lb. boneless pork shoulder roast, cubed
5 cloves garlic, minced
4 cans (14½ ounces each) diced tomatoes, undrained
8 cans (4 ounces each) diced green chilies, drained
1 green bell pepper, chopped
1 cup beef broth
2 tsp. cumin
½ tsp. sugar
¼ tsp. ground cloves
3 jalapeno peppers, seeded and chopped (optional)
⅓ cup fresh parsley, chopped

Heat the oil in a large Dutch oven or heavy pot. Brown the meat half at a time, adding garlic to the second half of the browning. Drain off the excess fat and return all of the meat to the Dutch oven.

Add remaining ingredients except for the parsley. Bring to a boil and then turn down the heat, cover the pot, and simmer for 2 hours, stirring occasionally.

Uncover and simmer for another 30 minutes or so until desired consistency. Stir in parsley just before serving.

Serves 4 to 6.

Clear Japanese Soup

For the soup:
3 quarts chicken broth
3 T. soy sauce

Garnishes:
12 to 14 small mushrooms, thinly sliced
2 bunches green onions, sliced diagonally ¼-inch thick
1 carrot, peeled and sliced paper thin
½ lb. small cooked shrimp
1 bunch cilantro, leaves pulled off stems

To make the soup: Bring the broth to a simmer; stir in soy sauce and continue to simmer for 5 minutes. Ladle into serving bowls.

Arrange the garnishes on a large serving tray or individual trays and serve along with the soup at the table. Offer more soy sauce as well.

Serves 6.

Creamy Beef Stew

2 T. oil
1½ lbs. beef stew meat, cubed
2 cups beef broth
1 clove garlic, minced
1 T. paprika
3 leeks (or 1 onion), chopped
½ lb. small button mushrooms
1 green or red bell pepper, seeded and chopped
1 T. cornstarch
2 T. apple juice
¼ cup heavy cream
Salt and pepper to taste

In a large Dutch oven or stockpot, heat the oil. Add the meat cubes and brown on all sides. Stir in the broth, minced garlic, and paprika. Bring to a boil and then cover the pot, reduce the heat, and simmer until the meat is tender, about 1 hour.

To prepare the leeks (if using): Cut off and discard the tops and very dark green portion. Cut the leeks lengthwise so you can rinse them well, and then slice them thickly.

If the mushrooms are small, you can leave them whole. If not, halve or thickly slice them.

Add all of the vegetables to the stew, bring to a boil, and then reduce the heat. Cover the pot and simmer until the vegetables are tender, about 20 minutes.

In a small bowl, combine the cornstarch and apple juice. Add to the cream and stir to mix.

After the vegetables are tender, increase the heat. Add the cream mixture while stirring constantly, and keep stirring until the mixture thickens slightly. Add salt and pepper to taste.

Serves 4 to 6.

SOUPS AND
STEWS

Creamy Salsify Soup

1½ cups salsify, peeled and sliced (see note below)
1½ cups water
1 T. butter
1 quart milk or half-and-half (or a combination)
Salt and pepper to taste
Parmesan cheese (optional)

Cook the salsify until tender in the water to which you have added a pinch of salt. Add the butter and milk or half-and-half and bring to nearly boiling. Season to taste and serve. Feel free to pass the Parmesan cheese at the table along with fresh, chopped parsley.

Serves 4.

Note: Salsify is also called "oyster plant" because of its vaguely similar taste to oysters. Salsify roots look a lot like carrots, except they are white or brown, depending on which variety you get. Scrub the roots before removing the skins and then remove any dark spots and trim the top and bottom of the roots before slicing. Also, salsify cooks faster than carrots, and it will become mushy if overcooked, so watch your pot carefully.

SOUPS AND STEWS

French Onion Soup

For the toast:
6 slices sourdough whole wheat baguette (needs to fit inside soup bowls for serving)
Butter, softened to room temperature
6 T. Parmesan cheese, grated

For the soup:
5 cups onion, thinly sliced
5 T. butter
1 T. olive oil
1 tsp. flour
1 tsp. salt
1 tsp. Dijon mustard
Pinch of pepper
6 cups beef stock or broth
1 cup dry sherry
⅓ cup Parmesan cheese, shredded
⅓ cup Gruyère cheese, shredded

To make the toast: Spread butter on the bread slices. Sprinkle each slice with 1 tablespoon of the grated Parmesan cheese. Toast the bread at 325° for 20 to 25 minutes or until nicely brown. Set aside to cool.

In a deep soup pot, sauté the onion in the butter and oil on low heat for about 40 minutes or until the onion is lightly browned and caramelized. Stir in the flour, salt, Dijon mustard, and pepper and cook for 2 to 3 minutes.

Pour in beef stock and sherry. Cook over medium heat, stirring, until the liquid boils; turn down heat and simmer for 30 minutes.

Transfer the soup to a large, flameproof casserole dish or tureen and sprinkle with the two cheeses. Put the casserole under a preheated broiler for 3 to 4 minutes or until the cheese is bubbly and just beginning to brown.

To serve, place a slice of toasted bread in each of 6 large soup bowls and divide the soup among them. Serve immediately.

Serves 6.

Note: Instead of preparing slices of toasted bread, when you're ready to eat, you can simply sprinkle some croutons over the top of the soup and add the cheese, which will melt as you eat the soup.

Green Curry Stew with Shrimp and Scallops

1 to 4 tsp. Thai green curry paste, depending on taste
1 can (about 13 ounces) coconut milk
1 T. olive or peanut oil
4 green onions cut into ½-inch pieces
1 red bell pepper, seeded and thinly sliced
2 cloves garlic, minced
½ tsp. ginger powder (1 T. minced fresh ginger)
½ lb. cooked shrimp
½ lb. small bay scallops (or omit the scallops and use 1 lb. cooked shrimp instead)
¼ cup fresh or frozen peas
1 tsp. lime or lemon juice, more or less depending on taste
¼ cup cilantro leaves

In a bowl, whisk together the curry paste and coconut milk.

Heat the oil in a saucepan and then add the green onions and bell pepper; sauté for 2 minutes, stirring often. Add the garlic and ginger and sauté for 1 minute, stirring gently.

Next, add the coconut milk mixture and heat until simmering. Add the shrimp, scallops, and peas. Reduce the heat, cover the pan, and simmer for about 3 to 5 minutes or until the scallops are opaque. Add the lime juice if using.

SOUPS AND STEWS

Serve in soup bowls and pass the cilantro for sprinkling. You can also serve the curry on top of a bed of hot, cooked brown rice or quinoa.

Serves 4.

Ground Turkey and Vegetable Soup

3 T. oil, divided
1 lb. ground turkey
4 cups chicken broth
6 cups water
½ cup lentils, rinsed and drained
½ cup pearled barley, rinsed and drained
½ onion, chopped
½ green bell pepper, diced
½ red bell pepper, diced
2 carrots, peeled and diced
1 celery stalk, diced
2 cloves garlic, minced
Salt and pepper to taste

In a large, heavy soup pot, heat 2 tablespoons of the oil over medium heat. Add the ground turkey and cook, breaking the meat into small pieces as you stir.

Add the broth, water, lentils, and barley. Bring to a boil and then reduce the heat. Cover and simmer for about 30 minutes.

In a skillet, heat 1 tablespoon of oil on medium-low. Add the onion, peppers, carrots, celery, and garlic and sauté the vegetables for about 5 minutes or until they begin to soften. Spoon the vegetable mixture into the soup pot. Bring to a boil and then reduce the heat. Cover and continue simmering for about 15 more minutes or until the lentils and barley are cooked through. Salt and pepper to taste and serve immediately.

Serves 6 to 8.

SOUPS AND STEWS

Notes:

172

Ground Turkey Chili

2 tsp. oil
1 onion, chopped
3 carrots, peeled and sliced or chopped
1 green bell pepper, seeded and chopped
1 cup fresh mushrooms, sliced
1 lb. ground turkey
2 tsp. oregano
1 to 2 T. chili powder or to taste
1 tsp. cumin
Pepper to taste
2 cans (28 ounces each) crushed tomatoes
1 tsp. hot pepper sauce (i.e. Tabasco or Cholula)
6 cloves garlic, minced
2 cans (15 ounces each) kidney or small red beans, rinsed and drained

In a large Dutch oven or heavy-bottom pot, heat the oil and sauté the onion, carrots, and bell peppers for 3 minutes. Add the mushrooms and cook 3 minutes more.

Add the turkey, oregano, chili powder, cumin, and pepper and cook, breaking up the ground turkey, until the meat is no longer pink. Add the remaining ingredients, stir well, and simmer over low heat for 30-45 minutes, stirring occasionally.

You can garnish individual bowls of stew with shredded cheese, a dollop of sour cream, and some fresh chopped parsley or cilantro if desired.

Serves 6 to 8.

Halibut Stew

½ green bell pepper, diced
2 T. onion, diced
1 clove garlic, minced
1 T. oil
1 large can (28 ounces) diced tomatoes, undrained
1 can (about 15 ounces) tomato sauce
1 zucchini, sliced or cubed (need about 1 cup)
¼ cup dry white wine
3 T. fresh parsley, minced
½ tsp. salt
¼ tsp. basil (or 1 tsp. fresh)
¼ tsp. thyme (or 1 tsp. fresh)
1 lb. halibut, cut into bite-sized pieces
1 cup shrimp (optional, but highly recommended)
1 cup clams (optional), minced

Sauté the bell peppers, onion, and garlic in the oil over medium heat, stirring, for several minutes.

Add the remaining ingredients except for the seafood. Bring to a gentle boil; reduce the heat to barely a simmer and cook for about 10 minutes.

Add the seafood and continue to simmer until the fish is cooked through, just a few minutes.

Serves 6 to 8.

Leek and Potato Soup with Bacon

8 slices bacon
3 medium white boiling potatoes, peeled
3 stalks celery
3 carrots, peeled
4 leeks
½ tsp. salt
Pepper to taste
2 cups milk or half-and-half

In a large, heavy pot, fry the bacon until crisp; remove the bacon, leaving the grease in the pot. (If there is too much, you can pour a little out.)

Finely chop the potatoes, celery, carrots, and leeks (use the white parts and just a bit of the lighter green parts) and place them in the pot containing the bacon grease along with the salt and pepper. Add just enough water to cover the vegetables and bring the contents of the pot to a boil. Reduce the heat and simmer for about 30 minutes, stirring occasionally and keeping careful watch that the pot doesn't boil dry. Add water if necessary to keep the vegetables barely covered. Do not drain.

Add the milk and heat thoroughly without boiling. Crumble the cooked bacon into the pot and serve.

Serves 4.

SOUPS AND
STEWS

Lentil Soup

5 cups water or broth
1 cup lentils, rinsed and picked over
1 onion, diced
2 stalks celery, diced
2 carrots, peeled and diced
1 clove garlic, minced
1 potato, peeled and diced
1 can (15 ounces) tomato sauce
½ tsp. curry powder
½ tsp. basil
Salt and pepper to taste

Place all of the ingredients except the salt and pepper in a large pot; bring to a boil and then reduce the heat. Cover the pot and simmer for 1 to 2 hours, stirring occasionally, or until the lentils are soft.

Serves 4 to 6.

Minestrone Soup

1 lb. beef shank
2½ quarts water
1 T. salt
1 cup dried white or red beans
1 T. olive oil
2 cloves garlic, minced
½ cup onion, minced
¼ cup fresh parsley
1 cup green beans, fresh or frozen, snapped into 1-inch pieces
1 potato, peeled and diced
¾ cup celery, diced
$^2/_3$ cup peas, fresh or frozen
2 cups cabbage, thinly shredded
1 cup carrots, diced
1 cup tomatoes, skinned and chopped
½ cup shell macaroni
Salt and pepper to taste
Parmesan cheese, shredded or grated, for garnish

Place the beef in a pot; add water, salt, and beans. Cover, bring to a boil, and then reduce the heat and simmer, stirring occasionally and skimming off fat, for 4 hours.

Remove the beef from the pot and allow it to cool enough to handle. Cut the meat into bite-sized pieces and set aside.

In a skillet, add the oil, garlic, onion, and parsley; sauté until tender but not brown. Add the onion mixture to the soup pot along with the green beans, potato, celery, peas, cabbage, carrots, and tomatoes. Cover and simmer for 30 minutes. Add the macaroni and beef and continue cooking until the macaroni is tender. Salt and pepper to taste and serve garnished with Parmesan cheese.

Serves 4 to 6.

SOUPS AND STEWS

Mushroom Soup with Parmesan Cheese

1 T. butter
1 T. olive oil
1 onion, finely diced
2 cloves garlic, peeled and cut in half lengthwise
1 lb. mushrooms, stems removed and thinly sliced
3 T. tomato paste
3 cups chicken broth
2 T. sweet vermouth
6 thick slices bread (Italian or sourdough)
Softened butter for spreading on bread slices
Salt and pepper to taste
Shredded Parmesan cheese to sprinkle on top of soup

In a heavy soup pot, melt the butter and add the oil. Then add the onion and garlic and brown gently; discard the garlic. Stir in the mushrooms and sauté for 5 to 10 minutes. Add the tomato paste and stir to mix well. Add the chicken broth and vermouth and stir well again. Bring to a gentle boil and then reduce the heat and simmer for 10 minutes.

While the soup is simmering, butter the bread and place it under the broiler to toast.

To serve, taste the soup and add salt and pepper to taste. Place one piece of toasted bread in the bottom of individual serving bowls, ladle the soup over the bread, and top with Parmesan cheese.

Serves 6.

SOUPS AND STEWS

Quick and Easy Taco Soup

1 lb. ground beef
1 small onion, chopped (or ½ large onion)
1 green bell pepper, chopped
1 can Ro-Tel diced tomatoes with chilies, undrained
2 cans (14.5 ounces each) diced tomatoes, undrained
3 cans water (use 4 cans if you like your soup "soupier")
1 T. powdered ranch dressing mix (or 1 packet of ranch dressing mix)
½ tsp. garlic powder
1 tsp. cumin
¼ cup brown rice
Salt and pepper to taste
Cheddar cheese for serving, shredded (optional)

In a large pot, brown the ground beef and then drain grease.

Return the meat to the pot and add the remaining ingredients. Bring to a boil, stirring regularly; reduce the heat and simmer until rice is cooked, about 50 minutes.

To serve, ladle into individual bowls and top with cheese.

Serves 4 to 6, although I've been known to get as many as 8 servings by adding more water.

Quick and Easy Tomato Soup

2 cans (6 ounces each) tomato paste
2 quarts water
2 stalks celery, chunked into thirds
½ tsp. salt
Pepper to taste
¼ tsp. onion powder
⅛ tsp. garlic powder
¼ tsp. oregano
¼ tsp. basil
¼ tsp. thyme
¼ tsp. rosemary
¼ tsp. celery seed (optional)
1 tsp. sugar
1 bay leaf (optional, but good)
¼ cup cream, half-and-half, or milk
Butter for garnish (optional)
Fresh parsley, minced, for garnish (optional)

In a large pot, combine all of the ingredients except the cream and garnishes. Stir to mix well. Bring to a low boil and then reduce the heat and simmer for 20 minutes. Remove the celery pieces and bay leaf. Taste and adjust seasonings if needed.

Pour in the cream and heat the soup until hot but not boiling. Serve with a small pat of butter and a sprinkling of minced parsley in each bowl if desired.

Serves 4 to 6.

SOUPS AND STEWS

Salmon Chowder

1 can (14¾ ounces) salmon
3 T. butter
1 clove garlic, minced
1 cup carrots, peeled and diced
½ cup onion, diced
½ cup celery, diced
½ cup green bell pepper, diced
½ cup potatoes, peeled and diced
2 cups chicken broth
1 tsp. salt
½ tsp. pepper
½ tsp. thyme
½ cup peas, fresh or frozen
1 cup corn, fresh or frozen
1 can evaporated milk
Fresh parsley, minced, for garnish (optional)

Drain and flake the salmon, reserving the liquid.

In a large pot, melt the butter. Add the garlic, carrots, onion, celery, bell pepper, and potatoes and sauté for several minutes or until they begin to cook and soften a bit.

Add the reserved salmon liquid, broth, salt, pepper, and thyme. Cover and simmer for 20 minutes.

Add the salmon, peas, corn, and evaporated milk and heat thoroughly. Garnish with minced fresh parsley if desired and serve immediately.

Serves 4 to 6.

SOUPS AND STEWS

Summertime Soup

1 T. oil
3 cloves garlic, minced
½ cup green onions, chopped
2 cups carrots, peeled and thinly sliced
2 cups asparagus, chopped (don't use the woody ends of the spears)
4 to 6 cups chicken or vegetable broth
4 T. lemon juice
¼ tsp. salt
⅛ tsp. pepper
1 cup spinach, Swiss chard, or watercress, torn
4 T. fresh parsley
Parmesan cheese, grated, for garnish

In a soup pot, heat the oil over medium heat. Add the garlic and sauté, stirring gently, for 1 minute. Add the green onions and carrots and continue cooking for about 5 minutes.

Next, add the asparagus, broth, lemon juice, salt, and pepper. Bring to a gentle simmer and cook just until the asparagus is tender but not overcooked. Add the spinach and parsley and then turn off the heat and let the greens wilt slightly, about 1 or 2 minutes.

Serve the soup with a small bowl of Parmesan cheese on the side for those who want to garnish.

Serves 6.

Sunflower Soup

6 cups chicken or vegetable broth
2 carrots, peeled and sliced
¼ cup onion, diced
½ cup sunflower seeds
Salt and pepper to taste
4 green onions, chopped, including some of the green parts

Place the chicken broth, carrots, and onion in a pot and bring to a boil. Reduce the heat and simmer for about 30 minutes.

Add the sunflower seeds and continue simmering for another 10 minutes. Add salt and pepper if desired and serve in bowls with some of the green onions sprinkled over the top.

Serves 6.

Turnip Soup

4 cups milk
1 onion, peeled and cut in half
2 T. butter
1 T. flour
2 cups grated turnips
1 tsp. salt
2 T. fresh parsley, chopped

In the top of a double boiler, add the milk and onion. Heat until it just begins to simmer, but don't let it come to a full boil.

Rub together the butter and flour to make a paste. Add the paste to the milk mixture while stirring. Add the grated turnips and salt, and cook while you continue stirring until the turnips are soft, about 10 minutes.

Just before serving, remove the onion and stir in the parsley.

Serves 6.

SOUPS AND
STEWS

Wild Rice and Chicken Soup

1 whole chicken, cooked (save the broth), deboned, and cut into bite-sized pieces
2 T. butter
½ cup onion, diced
¼ cup celery, chopped
½ cup fresh mushrooms, sliced
¼ cup flour
4 cups chicken broth from cooked chicken, or use store bought
2 cups cooked wild rice
1 can (8 ounces) water chestnuts, sliced
1 cup cream (or half-and-half)
¼ cup dry sherry (optional)

In a large heavy-bottom soup pot, melt the butter. Add the onion, celery, and mushrooms and sauté on medium-low heat, stirring regularly, for about 5 minutes or until the mixture is aromatic.

Stir in the flour and then gradually add the chicken broth, stirring constantly. Continue stirring until the mixture thickens somewhat. Stir in rice, water chestnuts, and cooked chicken and simmer for 5 minutes. Add the cream and sherry and heat to serving temperature and then serve immediately.

Serves 4 to 6.

Zucchini Soup

1 T. butter
2 cups zucchini, thinly sliced
½ cup onion, diced
1 tsp. lemon juice
2 cups chicken broth
1 cup heavy cream (or half-and-half)
Salt and pepper to taste

In a soup pot, melt the butter. Add the zucchini and onion and cook until the vegetables are tender, stirring gently but regularly.

Add the lemon juice and chicken broth and bring to a simmer. Cook, covered, for about 15 minutes. Reduce the heat slightly and add the cream. Heat thoroughly, but don't let it boil. Add salt and pepper to taste and serve.

Serves 4 to 6.

Note: You can enhance the flavor of this soup by adding a bit of garlic powder, thyme, summer savory, dill weed, rosemary, or basil.

SOUPS AND STEWS

VEGETABLES AND SIDES

Asparagus Italian Style ✓

1 lb. asparagus, woody stems trimmed
1 onion, chopped
1 large stalk celery, chopped
2 T. Parmesan cheese, shredded
2 T. bread crumbs
2 tomatoes, chopped
¼ tsp. thyme
¼ tsp. oregano

Preheat the oven to 350°.

Oil a baking dish with a small amount of olive oil, or spray it with cooking spray. Place the asparagus in a single layer in the bottom of the dish. Layer the remaining ingredients in the order listed above.

Cover tightly with aluminum foil and bake for 20 minutes or until the asparagus is crisp-tender.

Serves 4 to 6.

VEGETABLES AND SIDES

Baked Beets in Béchamel Sauce

4 medium beets, peeled and cut into ¼-inch-thick slices
½ cup water
3 T. butter
1 shallot, minced
3 T. flour
1 cup milk
¼ cup dry white wine
Salt and pepper to taste
Pinch of nutmeg

Preheat the oven to 425°.

Arrange the beets in a large baking dish. Add the water, cover tightly with aluminum foil, and bake for about 45 minutes or until the beets are fork tender.

Meanwhile, melt the butter in a saucepan over medium heat. Add the shallot and sauté until softened, about 3 minutes. Stir in the flour. Slowly whisk in the milk and wine, and then bring mixture to a gentle boil as it thickens.

Remove the sauce from the heat and add salt and pepper to taste and a pinch of nutmeg. Pour the sauce over the beets in the baking dish, and continue to bake, uncovered this time, for about 10 minutes or until the sauce is bubbling and golden brown around the edges.

Serves 4 to 6.

Baked Cornmeal Gnocchi ✓

4 cups milk
1 tsp. salt
Pinch of nutmeg
Pepper to taste
1 cup cornmeal or polenta
2 eggs
1 cup Parmesan cheese, grated, divided
¼ cup (½ stick) butter, melted

Using a deep, heavy saucepot, heat the milk to a boil. Add the salt, a pinch of nutmeg, and pepper to taste. Stirring constantly with a wooden spoon, gradually add the cornmeal or polenta. Cook over low heat, stirring, until well thickened, about ½ hour (the wooden spoon should be able to stand upright in the center). Remove the pot from the heat.

Beat the eggs lightly, combine with ¾ cup of the Parmesan cheese, and stir into cornmeal mixture.

Spread mixture in a large, buttered baking pan, about ¼-inch thick. Refrigerate until well chilled and firm.

Cut into 1½-inch rounds and place in an ovenproof baking dish, each overlapping the other in circles or rows. Dribble the melted butter over the top and sprinkle with the remaining cheese.

Bake in a preheated 400° oven for 15 minutes or until crispy and golden on top. Serve immediately.

Serves 6 to 8.

VEGETABLES
AND SIDES

Brussels Sprouts in Sour Cream Sauce √

 1 lb. brussels sprouts (smaller is better with brussels sprouts)
 ½ cup onion, chopped
 2 T. butter
 1 cup sour cream
 Salt and pepper to taste

Steam the brussels sprouts until tender, about 10 minutes; drain well.

Meanwhile, sauté the onion in the butter until tender, about 3 to 4 minutes. Add the sour cream and heat just until hot (but do not boil or the sour cream will curdle). Add the steamed sprouts and mix well. Add salt and pepper to taste and serve immediately.

Serves 6.

Brussels Sprouts with Dill Weed √

 1 lb. small brussels sprouts
 2 T. butter
 1 tsp. dried dill weed (or 2 T. fresh snipped dill weed)
 2 T. fresh chives, snipped

Remove any wilted or discolored leaves from the outside of the brussels sprouts, cut off the stem ends, and pierce the bottoms with a sharp knife to promote even cooking. Steam the brussels sprouts in a double boiler just until tender, about 5 minutes.

Melt the butter in a large skillet. Add the brussels sprouts, dill weed, and chives. Sauté over medium-high heat, stirring regularly, for 2 minutes.

Serves 6.

Cauliflower, Broccoli, and Spinach Baked in Béchamel Sauce ✓

2½ cups cauliflower florets
2½ cups broccoli florets
12 ounces baby spinach leaves
6 T. (¾ stick) butter
½ cup flour
²/₃ cup milk
²/₃ cup Parmesan cheese, shredded

Cook the cauliflower and broccoli in a large pot of boiling water for 5 minutes; drain, reserving ⅔ cup of the cooking liquid. Place the cooked vegetables in a large mixing bowl and let cool.

Rinse the spinach and immediately place it in a large skillet set on medium-high heat. Stir as needed, cooking the spinach just until it wilts; drain spinach. When cool enough to handle, squeeze the spinach to release more liquid and then chop.

In a heavy pot, melt the butter. Add flour and, stirring constantly, gradually add the milk and reserved vegetable cooking liquid. Continue to cook and stir until the sauce boils and thickens. Remove from heat; stir in cheese, stirring so it mostly melts, and then stir in the chopped spinach.

Coarsely crumble the cauliflower and broccoli in the large bowl. Add the spinach cheese sauce, and then add salt and pepper to taste and spoon the mixture into a buttered baking dish.

Bake in a preheated 350° oven for 25 minutes or until bubbly and lightly browned on top.

Serves 8 to 10.

VEGETABLES AND SIDES

Cauliflower "Mashed Potatoes" ✓

1 head cauliflower, coarsely chopped
1 tsp. olive oil
Salt and pepper to taste

Steam the cauliflower until tender, about 10 minutes. Mash the cauliflower, olive oil, and salt and pepper until relatively smooth. Serve.

You can also add a bit of garlic, butter, or 1 tablespoon of minced chipotle chili pepper canned in adobo sauce for tasty variations.

Yield varies depending on size of cauliflower.

Celery with Almonds

3 T. butter
4 cups celery, cut in very thin 3-inch long strips
2 T. chives, minced
½ cup green onions, finely chopped
1 small clove garlic, minced
½ cup slivered almonds, toasted

Using a heavy skillet, melt the butter and add the celery. Cook over low heat for about 3 minutes, stirring constantly.

Add the chives, green onions, and garlic. Cook a bit longer, still stirring constantly, but do not overcook. The celery should be somewhat crisp when served.

To serve, combine the celery mixture and toasted almonds, reserving a small amount of the almonds to sprinkle on top.

Serves 6 to 8.

Notes:

VEGETABLES AND SIDES

Colorful Quinoa ✓

1½ cups vegetable broth
1 cup quinoa, thoroughly rinsed and drained
½ tsp. salt
½ tsp. pepper
1 cup frozen mixed vegetables
    (such as peas, carrots, green beans, and corn)

In a medium saucepan, bring the broth to a boil over medium-high heat. Stir in the quinoa, salt, and pepper. Reduce the heat to low, cover the saucepan with a tight-fitting lid, and cook until the broth is absorbed and the quinoa is tender, about 15 minutes.

Turn off the heat, remove the lid, and stir in the vegetables. Return the lid to the saucepan and allow the quinoa to sit on the stove for several minutes to heat the vegetables. Fluff and stir with a fork and serve immediately.

Serves 6.

Cornmeal Bites with Basil Butter ✓

4 cups water
2 tsp. salt
1⅓ cups cornmeal
3 T. butter
1 clove garlic, minced
1 tsp. dried basil
2 T. Parmesan cheese, grated

Lightly grease a large jelly roll pan (the kind that has sides all the way around).

In a medium saucepan, bring the water and salt to a boil. Whisk in the cornmeal, stirring constantly so it doesn't form lumps. Simmer gently for about 10 minutes, stirring often, until so thick that a spoon can stand up in the mixture, but it's still pourable.

Spread the hot cornmeal evenly in the prepared pan and smooth with a rubber or silicone spatula. Put the pan in the refrigerator and chill for at least an hour or until firm.

Once the pan is chilled and ready to bake, preheat the oven to 425°.

Melt the butter in a small saucepan or in the microwave in a small microwavable container. Stir in the garlic and basil.

Invert the cornmeal onto a clean work surface and cut into about 35 squares. Arrange half of the squares on the jelly roll pan. Drizzle or brush half of the butter mixture across the top, and sprinkle with half of the Parmesan cheese.

Bake for 20 to 25 minutes or until the edges are crisp. Keep the first batch warm, either in a warming oven or by covering the squares with a towel while you bake the second batch. When the second batch is done, quickly reheat the first batch in the still-hot oven and then serve the squares hot, either as an appetizer or a side dish.

Yields 35 squares.

Cucumber Cream Cheese Cups

2 English cucumbers (English cucumbers have fewer, smaller seeds and are about 12 inches long)
1 package (8 ounces) cream cheese
¼ cup onion, diced
1 T. fresh dill weed (or 1 tsp. dried)
1 T. milk
⅛ tsp. salt
⅛ tsp. pepper
2 T. pistachio nuts, minced

Peel the cucumbers and cut each crosswise into 8 chunks. Using a melon baller or spoon, carefully hollow out one cut end to make a cup shape. Set the cucumber cups on several layers of paper towels, hollowed side down, to drain while making the filling.

In a small mixing bowl, use a sturdy fork to combine the cream cheese, onion, dill weed, milk, salt, and pepper. (It will be easier to get a smooth filling if you allow the cream cheese to sit out for about 20 minutes to soften.)

Turn the cucumber cups so the hollows are upright and spoon the filling inside. When ready to serve, sprinkle the tops with the pistachio nuts.

Yields 16 pieces.

Eggplant, Zucchini, and Tomato √ Casserole

1 lb. eggplant
1 lb. zucchini
2 cups water
2 tsp. salt
¼ cup (½ stick) butter
1 large onion, diced
¾ lb. tomatoes, skinned and chopped
Salt and pepper to taste
1¼ cups cheddar cheese, shredded

Peel the eggplant. Cut in half lengthwise, slice ½-inch thick, and then turn and slice ½-inch thick crosswise. Slice the zucchini diagonally ½-inch thick.

Place the eggplant and zucchini in a large pot with the water and salt. Cook, covered, 7 to 8 minutes. Drain well and set the vegetables aside.

In the same pot, melt the butter, add the diced onion, and sauté until tender, about 15 minutes. Remove from the heat. This is also a good time to preheat the oven to 350°.

VEGETABLES
AND SIDES

Add the vegetables and tomatoes. Mix gently as you don't want to break the pieces. Add salt and pepper to taste.

Place the mixture in a fairly shallow baking dish that has been well greased or buttered. Sprinkle the cheese evenly over the top and bake in the oven, covered tightly with aluminum foil, for 30 minutes. Remove foil and bake uncovered for 5 minutes more to evaporate liquid.

Serves 6.

Fresh Spinach Dip

1 lb. fresh spinach
½ cup fresh parsley
½ cup green onions (or regular onion)
½ tsp. dill weed
1 cup mayonnaise
1 cup sour cream
1 tsp. seasoned salt
1 T. lemon juice

Set a large pot or bowl into a sink filled about halfway with ice cubes; add cold water to just cover the ice cubes.

Blanch the spinach by putting the leaves into a large pot of boiling water for about 30 seconds to 1 minute. Quickly remove the spinach from the boiling water using a slotted spoon, or pour out the mixture through a colander so the water drains and the spinach is caught, making sure to keep the boiling water away from the iced water.

Place the blanched spinach in the container in the ice water and let cool. Drain the cooled spinach and squeeze it dry. Chop the spinach and put it in another bowl. Add the rest of the ingredients and mix well. Refrigerate for 24 hours before serving with fresh veggies, sourdough bread, or crackers.

Yields about 4 cups.

Homemade Cottage Cheese

1 gallon milk
⅓ cup white vinegar
Heavy-duty, tight-weave cheesecloth
Salt to taste

Pour the milk into a large, nonreactive pot such as stainless steel and slowly heat the milk to 180° to 190°. (There's no need to stir, but you do need to heat slowly for best results.)

When the milk has reached the proper temperature, remove from heat and add the vinegar. Stir to mix and then let the mixture set for about 30 minutes or until the curds and whey completely separate.

Pour the curds and whey into a large colander that has been lined with a double thickness of cheesecloth. Allow the whey to drain completely, about 30 minutes. From time to time while it's draining, lift the cheesecloth bundle to get the whey draining well again as the colander can clog.

When the draining seems complete, wrap the cheesecloth around the curds and rinse with cool tap water for several minutes, gently kneading the curds as you rinse (while being careful not to smash them). After rinsing, allow the curds to drain again while still in the cheesecloth bundle, about 15 minutes or so.

Place the rinsed and drained curds in a bowl, add some cream or half-and-half if you like creamier cottage cheese, and salt to taste.

Yields about 3 cups.

VEGETABLES
AND SIDES

Homemade Ricotta Cheese

Heavy-duty, tight-weave cheesecloth
2 quarts (½ gallon) whole milk
1 cup heavy cream
½ tsp. salt
3 T. lemon juice

Line a large sieve or fine-mesh colander with a layer of the cheesecloth and place it over a large bowl.

In a heavy-bottom pot, slowly bring the milk, cream, and salt to a rolling boil over moderate heat, stirring regularly so the bottom doesn't scorch. Add the lemon juice, reduce the heat to low, and simmer, stirring constantly, until the mixture curdles, about 2 to 3 minutes.

Carefully pour the mixture into the prepared sieve or colander and let drain for 1 hour. When completely drained, chill the ricotta, covered. Will keep for about 2 days in the refrigerator.

Yields about 2 cups.

Homemade Sour Cream

Note: Because store-bought milk is pasteurized with high-heat treatment, you need to use a starter culture in this recipe. Also, if you want "light" sour cream, use milk instead of half-and-half, but you'll end up with a creamier version when using half-and-half.

1 quart pasteurized half-and-half
1 packet direct-set sour cream starter culture

In a heavy-bottom saucepan, heat the cream to 86°. Stir in the starter and then let the cream sit undisturbed at room temperature (about 72°) for 12 hours, or until coagulated.

It is now ready to use. Refrigerate for up to a week.

Yields 1 quart.

Hungarian Cucumbers

2 large cucumbers
½ cup sour cream
3 T. mayonnaise
1 to 3 tsp. paprika
3 tsp. lemon juice
Salt and pepper to taste

Peel the cucumbers, cut lengthwise in half, and scoop out the seeds. Slice the cucumbers into thin slices.

Combine the remaining ingredients and gently toss with the cucumbers. Chill well before serving.

Yields about 3 cups.

Onions Filled with Broccoli

3 large sweet onions, with outer papery skin peeled
1 lb. fresh broccoli
½ cup Parmesan cheese, shredded
⅓ cup mayonnaise
2 tsp. lemon juice

Preheat the oven to 375°.

Cut the onions in half crosswise. Gently parboil them in salted water for 10 to 12 minutes; drain.

Remove the centers of the onions, leaving ¾-inch walls. Do not be concerned if some of the onions come apart during parboiling as they can easily be reassembled. Chop the center portions of the onions to equal 1 cup and set aside.

Cook the broccoli in boiling salted water until just tender. Chop the tender tops and combine them with the chopped onion, Parmesan cheese, mayonnaise, and lemon juice.

Mound the broccoli mixture in the onion halves. Place them in a buttered, shallow casserole dish or large pie plate and bake, uncovered, for 20 minutes.

Serves 6.

Ricotta Parmesan Squares

1 container (15 ounces) ricotta cheese
2 T. plus ¼ cup Parmesan cheese, shredded, divided
2 tsp. flour
¼ tsp. marjoram

Preheat the oven to 425°.

In a medium bowl, combine the ricotta cheese, 2 tablespoons of the Parmesan cheese, flour, and marjoram. Mix well.

Spread the mixture in an ungreased 8- or 9-inch square pan; sprinkle with the remaining ¼ cup Parmesan cheese.

Bake for 20 minutes or until the top is golden brown. Cool for 5 minutes before cutting into 16 squares and serving.

Yields 16 pieces.

Roasted Asparagus

2 lbs. asparagus
4 cloves garlic, minced
Olive oil
Salt and pepper to taste

Preheat the oven to 400°.

Break off woody ends of the asparagus. (Place your hands on each end of a spear and bend the ends down—the asparagus will break at just the right spot.)

Lay the spears in a single layer on a baking sheet. Sprinkle them with the minced garlic and a drizzle of olive oil.

Place the asparagus in the oven and shake the pan (or use a spatula or tongs) to turn the asparagus about every 4 or 5 minutes. Continue baking and turning the asparagus until the spears begin to wrinkle and have spots of brown, about 15 minutes, depending on how dark of a roast you prefer.

Remove from the oven, season with salt and pepper, and serve. They are good as is, or you can drizzle a bit of balsamic vinegar over them, or dip them in mayonnaise when eating.

Serves 6 to 8.

Roasted Brussels Sprouts with Bacon and Feta

3 slices bacon, diced
1½ lbs. brussels sprouts
2 cloves garlic (or ¼ tsp. garlic powder)
Salt and pepper to taste
4 T. Feta cheese crumbles
Balsamic vinegar (optional)

Preheat the oven to 400°.

Fry the bacon pieces until limp and some of the grease has rendered out. Remove with a slotted spoon and set aside.

Trim the brussels sprouts and take off any damaged leaves. Cut larger sprouts in half, but leave the small sprouts whole.

Lightly oil a baking pan. Combine the brussels sprouts, bacon, garlic, salt, and pepper. Place in prepared baking pan and roast for 25 to 30 minutes, flipping the sprouts about halfway through.

When the brussels sprouts are lightly browned and the bacon is crisp, remove from the oven and sprinkle on the Feta cheese.

VEGETABLES AND SIDES

Notes:

Mix gently, drizzle on a small amount of balsamic vinegar if using, and serve immediately.

Serves 6.

Roasted Brussels Sprouts with Hazelnuts and Parmesan

3 T. butter
½ tsp. salt
½ tsp. pepper
1½ lbs. brussels sprouts, trimmed and quartered lengthwise
¼ cup chopped hazelnuts
2 T. Parmesan cheese, shredded

Preheat the oven to 450°.

In a small saucepan, melt the butter until bubbling but not too brown. Remove from the heat and stir in the salt and pepper.

Place the brussels sprouts and hazelnuts in a lightly greased baking dish; drizzle the melted butter over the sprouts and hazelnuts and gently toss to coat. Roast for 12 to 15 minutes or until the sprouts are tender, stirring occasionally.

Remove from the oven and immediately sprinkle with Parmesan cheese.

Serves 6.

Roasted Vegetables with Lime and Pine Nuts

2 zucchinis, chunked
½ onion, cut into wedges
1 large tomato, cut in half and then each half cut into wedges
4 small fingerling or red potatoes, whole if small or cut in half if larger
8 button mushrooms, cut in half
2 carrots, peeled and chunked
½ cup eggplant, peeled and chunked
½ cup chopped bell pepper
3 T. pine nuts
2 cloves garlic, minced
½ tsp. thyme
2 tsp. olive oil, more or less
⅛ cup lime juice (or to taste)
Salt and pepper to taste

Note: I cut my vegetable pieces larger than bite-sized as they tend to roast better.

Preheat the oven to 400°.

Lightly spray a large jelly roll pan with cooking spray.

In a gallon-size plastic freezer bag, place the vegetables, pine nuts, garlic, and thyme. Drizzle a small amount of olive oil into the bag—about 2 teaspoons should be plenty. Close the top of the freezer bag and then gently mix the ingredients. Pour contents of bag into the prepared jelly roll pan. Drizzle the lime juice over the vegetables, being careful to coat thoroughly.

Roast for about 15 minutes in the oven. Gently turn the vegetables and continue to roast until the edges begin to brown and the vegetables are crisp-tender, about another 10 to 15 minutes, depending on the size of the chunks. If the vegetables start getting too dark, turn down the oven to 325° and continue to roast just until vegetables are crisp-tender.

VEGETABLES
AND SIDES

You can substitute other vegetables if you desire. Also, try roasted vegetable sandwiches by spreading toasted hoagie rolls with a bit of mayonnaise and then piling on the roasted veggies. So good!

Serves 6.

Sautéed Kohlrabi

1½ lbs. kohlrabi bulbs
2 T. butter
½ cup chicken broth
1 tsp. fresh tarragon, minced (or ½ tsp. dried tarragon)
Salt and pepper to taste
½ cup fresh parsley, minced (optional)

Using a sharp knife, trim and peel the kohlrabi. Cut the bulbs into strips about ¼-inch thick.

Sauté the kohlrabi in the butter, stirring to coat the strips. Stir in the broth and tarragon and then cover and cook until tender, about 10 minutes or so. Remove the cover and continue cooking until the kohlrabi takes on a golden color.

Add salt and pepper to taste and then sprinkle with the parsley, if using, just before serving.

Serves 4 to 6.

Sautéed Swiss Chard

6 stalks Swiss chard (rainbow chard, often called Neon Lights, is beautiful
  in this recipe)
1 T. olive oil
1 tsp. butter
¼ cup onion, chopped
¼ cup dry white wine
Salt and pepper to taste
1 roma tomato, diced (optional)
4 T. Parmesan cheese, shredded (or to taste)

Clean and separate the Swiss chard stalks from the leaves. Chop the stalks and leaves, keeping them separate.

Add the oil and butter to a sauté pan and heat on medium. Add the onion and stalks of chard and sauté, stirring occasionally, for about 4 minutes. Add the wine, chopped leaves, salt and pepper and continue cooking, stirring occasionally, for another 3 minutes. Remove from the heat.

Sprinkle the diced tomatoes if using and the Parmesan cheese over the top. Cover the pan and allow the chard to rest for a minute or two so the Parmesan cheese melts a bit.

Serves 4.

Scalloped Eggplant

1 large eggplant, peeled
6 slices bacon
3 eggs
1 cup milk
2 cups whole wheat bread, crusts removed and cubed
1 cup cheddar cheese, shredded
1 T. butter
½ cup Parmesan cheese, grated

Cut the eggplant into 1-inch cubes and boil in a large pot of water for 2 minutes. Drain the eggplant well, patting the cubes dry with paper towels.

In a frying pan, fry the bacon slices until just barely crisp. Remove from the heat and cut or tear the bacon into 1-inch pieces.

In a large mixing bowl, beat together the eggs and milk and then add the eggplant, bacon, bread cubes, and cheddar cheese and gently mix.

Pour the eggplant mixture into a buttered, ovenproof casserole dish and dot with the butter. Sprinkle the Parmesan cheese evenly over the top and bake at 325° for 30 to 40 minutes or until set and golden on top.

Yield varies depending on the size of the eggplant, but usually about 6 servings.

Scalloped Green Beans

1 lb. green beans, fresh or frozen
8 slices bacon
1 cup cheddar cheese, shredded
3 eggs
1½ cups half-and-half
½ tsp. salt
¼ tsp. pepper
Nutmeg (optional)

Preheat the oven to 325°.

If using fresh green beans, steam blanch them for 1 minute and then drain. If using frozen green beans, boil them for 1 to 2 minutes, or until thawed, and drain.

Fry the bacon until crisp; set aside to drain on paper towels.

Butter a rectangular baking dish and evenly spread out the beans across the bottom. Crumble the cooked bacon evenly over the beans and then sprinkle with the cheddar cheese.

In a mixing bowl, whisk the eggs until smooth and then add the half-and-half, salt, and pepper and combine all ingredients well. Pour mixture over the green beans and then sprinkle with nutmeg if using.

Bake for about 25 minutes or until the beans are cooked through and tender and the top is golden brown.

Serves 6 to 8.

VEGETABLES AND SIDES

Spicy Sautéed Broccoli ✓

1 bunch broccoli
4 T. oil
2 cloves garlic, peeled
1 to 2 T. red pepper flakes (or crushed red pepper)
Salt and pepper to taste

Remove stalks from broccoli and cut the remainder into 1½-inch pieces.

Heat the oil in a large skillet and add the garlic cloves. Stir and cook on medium heat for about 2 minutes. Remove garlic and discard it.

Add broccoli and red pepper flakes. Stir and then cover and cook over low heat until the broccoli is bright green and crisp tender (about 5 minutes), adding a tablespoon or two of water if necessary so broccoli doesn't burn. Stir occasionally.

Serves 4.

Spinach Soufflé Stuffed Mushrooms ✓

1-1½ lbs. large button mushroom caps
1 package (about 12 ounces) frozen spinach soufflé, thawed
Parmesan cheese, shredded or grated

Preheat the oven to 375°.

Remove the stems and part of the meat from the mushrooms. Place them in a buttered casserole dish with the cavities up and their sides touching (it helps the mushrooms to stay upright).

Spoon the spinach soufflé into the mushroom caps, mounding the soufflé. Sprinkle each with some Parmesan cheese.

Bake for 20 to 25 minutes or until the soufflé is completely cooked and slightly puffed.

Serves 4 to 6.

Sugar Smart Ketchup

Note: This version of ketchup contains no sugar. It's different from store-bought, but tasty.

2 cans (6 ounces each) tomato paste (make sure the only ingredient is tomatoes)
4 T. apple cider vinegar
1 T. regular mustard
¼ cup water
½ tsp. salt
½ tsp. cinnamon
⅛ tsp. cloves
¼ tsp. garlic powder

Combine all ingredients and mix until very well blended. If the ketchup seems too thick, you can add a tablespoon or two of water to thin it. Refrigerate for several hours or overnight to give the flavors a chance to meld. It will keep for several weeks if stored in the refrigerator in a container with a tight-fitting lid.

Yields about ¾ of a cup.

Note: You can use this in place of store-bought ketchup, but it's also tasty as a dip for vegetables.

Tomatoes with Pine Nuts and Parsley

6 tomatoes
2 T. olive oil
½ cup pine nuts
4 T. butter
2 to 3 cloves garlic, minced
1 cup fresh parsley, minced

Halve and seed the tomatoes (it's not necessary to get out all the seeds). Sprinkle the cut sides with a small amount of salt and then let them drain cut side down for 15 to 30 minutes.

VEGETABLES AND SIDES

When they have drained sufficiently, preheat the oven to 350°. Sauté the tomatoes in the olive oil for 2 to 3 minutes on each side, or until they are beginning to soften. Set them cut side up in an ovenproof baking dish (the size will vary depending on how big your tomatoes are) and keep them warm in the oven.

Pour the olive oil that you just used to sauté the tomatoes into a small skillet and turn the heat to medium. Add the pine nuts and sauté for about 2 minutes or until they are lightly colored. Transfer them with a slotted spoon to paper towels to drain.

In a medium skillet, melt the butter and then add the garlic and minced parsley plus a pinch of salt. Sauté, gently stirring often, for 5 minutes.

Remove the tomatoes from the oven and spoon the parsley mixture over the tomatoes; top them with the pine nuts. They are ready to serve immediately, or you can return them to the oven for about 5 minutes if they need a bit more cooking time.

Serves 6 to 12.

RECIPE INDEX

Breads, Crackers, and Rolls

Breakfast and Brunch

Desserts

Grains and Noodles

Lunches and Light Fare

Main Dishes and Casseroles

Salads and Salad Dressings

Soups and Stews

Vegetables and Sides